Newnes Technical Books

is an imprint of the Butterworth Group
which has principal offices in
London, Boston, Durban, Singapore, Sydney, Toronto, Wellington

First published 1982
Reprinted 1984 (with revision)

British Library Cataloguing in Publication Data

Parr, E. A.
  Beginner's guide to microprocessors.
  1. Microprocessors
  I. Title
  621.3819'5835   TK7895.M5

  ISBN 0-408-00579-3

Typeset by Butterworths Litho Preparation Department
Printed in England by Whitstable Litho Ltd, Whitstable, Kent.

Preface

Few devices have received the publicity that has accompanied the arrival of the microcomputer. Unfortunately, overstated press reports of its capabilities and gloomy forecasts from social scientists have left most people somewhat bemused.

This book deals with the microprocessor factually and describes its uses, abilities and shortcomings. In a book of this size it is not possible to deal with all related topics. Further details on general computing can be found in the companion book 'Beginner's Guide to Computers', and details of the manufacturing processes involved in making a microprocessor in 'Beginner's Guide to Integrated Circuits'.

This book is designed for the beginner, and assumes little of its reader beyond an interest in the subject. It is hoped that the book will transform this interest to the point where the reader acquires his (or her) own machine. If there is to be a second industrial revolution, it should be one in which we all take a part.

There are many firms and individuals who have assisted with this book. First there are all the semiconductor manufacturers who provided information on their products, and in particular Zilog who allowed the detailed descriptions of the Z-80 and Z-8000 to be used for illustrative purposes. It should be noted that all the microprocessor names are registered trade marks.

Considerable assistance was also given by many micro-computer users. GEC, Commodore, Scomagg, Hall Automation, M & B Games, Lambertons and BSC all freely gave information on applications.

On a personal level, there is my wife, who (in the age of the word processor) converted my illegible handwriting into typewritten text (and continues to tolerate the computer in the dining room). Finally, my eldest son Nicky, who (somewhat reluctantly) allowed me to disassemble his 'Big Trak'.

Andrew Parr

Dedication

For Nicky, Jamie and Simon
who will grow up with the microcomputer

Acknowledgement

The publishers wish to thank Compshop, 14 Station Road, New Barnet, Herts EN5 1QW for the loan of the UK101 shown on the cover.

Contents

'There is nothing more difficult to take in hand, more perilous to conduct, or more uncertain in its success, than to take the lead in the introduction of a new order of things, because the innovator has for enemies all those who have done well under the old conditions, and lukewarm defenders in those who may do well under the new. This coolness arises partly from fear of the opponents who have laws on their side, and partly from the incredulity of men, who do not readily believe in new things until they have a long experience of them.'

The Prince, Machiavelli

1

Introduction to computers

Myths and fallacies

There can be very few people who are unaware of the existence of a remarkable device called a microprocessor. Unfortunately most people have learned of the device from the popular media in one form or another, and the usual presentations are emotive and sensational rather than factual.

Women's magazines give a charming view of the housewife of the future sitting comfortably while the robot butler does the housework, the robot gardener mows the lawn and the robot kitchen chooses (and prepares) the evening meal with regard for family preferences and nutritional requirements.

Newspapers report, with morbid glee, on the effect of the microprocessor on employment. An M.P. states that 'One chip is worth, oh I don't know how many hundred people'. A union newspaper is more precise (but equally incorrect) when it says that 'One microprocessor will replace 800 jobs'.

Social scientists, of course, have had a field day, and scarcely a day goes past without hearing, or reading, 'A report out today states that . . . .' followed by some gloomy analysis of the effect of the microprocessor on human life. At times it seems that less material is written about the use of computers than about their social implications.

Advertisements also add to the confusion, and anything containing more than a handful of transistors has a 'microchip'. We thus have the computer watch, the computer oven, the computer car engine and the computer TV game. Some of the claims are true, most are not.

All of the above reports are, of course, widely inaccurate, overstate the capability of the microprocessor and confuse computers with integrated circuits (a related, but totally independent branch of electronics). Given such exaggerated stories it is not surprising that most people are totally confused and slightly apprehensive about the microprocessor and its impact on their lives.

Much of this confusion can be avoided by adopting a sceptical attitude and realising that most TV and newspaper reporters are only marginally better informed than their public, and very often what is presented is merely a garbled third-hand version of a press release that was overstated in the first place.

Quite often this ignorance shows through with bizarre results. The press, for example, has still to learn of the difference between silicon and silicone. Distinct lack of research was also displayed when articles were written about the UK firm INMOS and its 64K RAM chip (see Chapter 2 for a description of RAMs). One paper described it as 'a chip with 64 000 uses'. A quality daily solemnly asserted that 'a few years ago a chip of this complexity would have been called a computer'. Some sort of award, however, should go to the newspaper whose reporter wrote of 'the UK firm EXMOS who have devised a chip which will store 64 kilogrammes'.

Most of the popular beliefs about the microprocessor are fallacious. Some of the more common are:

a. The microprocessor is a special computer. Wrong; a microprocessor is an integrated circuit comprising one small part of a conventional computer. As we shall see, many additional integrated circuit packages (i.c.p.s) are needed to make a computer. A computer using a microprocessor is called a microcomputer.

b. A microcomputer is a superior superbrain computer. Wrong; most of the minicomputers, (and all the large mainframe computers) of the last decade are considerably more powerful than any microcomputer.

2

c. Microcomputers are very cheap. This is partly true, and it is certainly possible to buy a home computer for the same price as a reasonable hi-fi system but this is not the whole story. In any commercial or industrial computer system the actual cost of the computer has always been a small part of the total cost. The majority of the cost has always been the human effort in the design and programming of the system. This will not change and programming costs could even increase as microcomputers are not as versatile as their larger brethren. The only applications where computer costs will fall are those where the programming costs can be shared amongst several customers. The biggest market in this category is probably program packages for small businesses.

d. Microprocessors lead to unemployment. This is partially true, but it is more accurate to say that they will lead to a change in employment patterns. The choice is not between full employment without microprocessors, and unemployment with microprocessors. The real choice is between some unemployment with microprocesors and even more unemployment without.

In this book the microprocessor is described factually, and its strengths and weaknesses are outlined. Before we can describe the microprocessor, however, we must first describe the operation of a typical computer because the microcomputer is really no different from any other computer.

The human computer

From the early nineteenth century until the middle of this century there existed an actual job called a 'computer'. Computers were skilled in basic arithmetic and were employed by engineering firms, universities and similar organisations to perform lengthy mathematical calculations for engineers and scientists.

A computer would sit in an office with the equipment in *Fig. 1.1*, his connections with the outside world being his in-tray and his out-tray. An engineer requiring, say, the calculation of the strain in different girders in a bridge would write out a set of instructions and drop them with the relevant drawings, into the in-tray. Because the computers generally only had the most elementary engineering knowledge the instructions would be a step-by-step list so that the computer did not really need to know what he was doing. (Many people asserted this was desirable to prevent the computers taking short cuts on their own initiative.) The computer would then perform the necessary calculations and put the results in his out-tray for later collection.

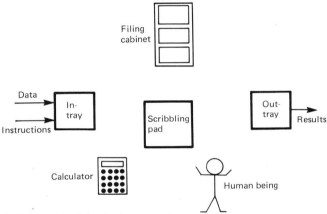

Figure 1.1. The job of a 'computer'

The equipment used by the computer is fairly obvious. The in-tray and out-tray have already been described. A calculator is needed to perform arithmetical calculations. When the job of computer was in being, the only calculators available were mechanical machines capable of addition and subtraction. Multiplication and division had to be done by repeated addition or subtraction. It is interesting to note that most microcomputers have a similar restriction.

The next item is not so obvious; a scribbling pad. During the course of the calculation the computer needed to record part results and other data for use later. The scribbling pad was thus used as a temporary store for data.

4

In many calcualtions the computer would require access to standard information. In a bridge calculation, for example, he would require dimensional information on standard girder sizes. This information would be required infrequently and could best be stored in some form of filing system.

Finally there was the computer himself, who read the instructions and controlled the equipment to produce the desired result.

A formal list of the equipment needed to perform the job of a 'computer' would therefore be:

a. An input medium for data and instructions.

b. An output medium for results.

c. A number cruncher for arithmetic calculations. This can be quite rudimentary with only addition and subtraction if the time penalty of using laborious routines for multiplication and division can be accepted.

d. A storage system for temporary data. Fast and convenient access to this data will be needed.

e. A storage system for instructions. Again, fast and convenient access will be required to the instructions. Usually instructions and temporary data are stored in the same manner. In the historical job example, paper is used. As will be seen, an electronic computer uses an electronic store called a RAM (Random Access Memory).

f. A bulk storage system for data required infrequently. Access to this data can be relatively slow. This bulk storage needs to be organised and indexed so that the required data can be found, used and replaced.

g. Some form of control to read the instructions, decide what to do next and manipulate the rest of the equipment. In the job of 'computer' this was a human being.

In the early part of the nineteenth century an engineer called Charles Babbage was involved in the production of nautical tables for the Admiralty. This involved vast teams of computers working under the direction of scientists and astronomers. The results were often incorrect, with disastrous results for the navy and its ships, and Babbage considered that it should be possible to mechanise the procedure. He correctly identified the seven items in the list above, and designed a mechanical computer which he termed an Analytical Engine. Sadly, Babbage had correctly worked out the requirements for a modern computer, but the technology of his time could not build it. The implementation of Babbage's ideas had to wait over a hundred years for the establishment of the electronics industry in the middle of this century.

The electronic computer

All computers ever built are based on Babbage's ideas, and are similar to the block diagram of *Fig. 1.2.* Each block on this diagram corresponds to one item on the list above. The connections to the outside world, for example, are made via the input unit and output unit. For the human computer the

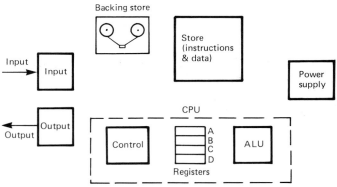

Figure 1.2. The electronic computer

communication was by paper. Electronic computers do often produce printed outputs, but the range of communication devices is very wide. Inputs can come from keyboards, punched tape, punched cards and, in the case of control computers, sensors such as limit switches and thermocouples. Outputs can be to printers, punched tape, TV screens or actuators such as hydraulic valves, motors or relays.

The heart of the computer is probably the store, which is used to hold both the instructions to be followed and the data to be processed. It is important to realise that everything in the store is held in the form of numbers. Instructions, numerical data, and alphabetical data are all held in the same form and the store does not differentiate between them.

A computer store can best be considered as an array of pigeon-holes similar to *Fig. 1.3*. Each pigeon-hole (called a

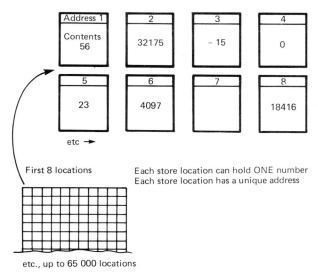

Figure 1.3. The store

'location') can hold one number (called somewhat confusingly a 'word'), and each pigeon-hole has an address by which it can be identified in a similar manner to house numbers in a street. If the store has, say, 4096 locations, the first location will have address 0, the second address 1 and so on up to address 4095. Most computer stores have over 16 000 locations.

The human computer needed a calculator, and one is provided in the electronic computer. This is the block labelled ALU (for Arithmetic and Logic Unit). The ALU contains an electronic circuit to perform addition and subtraction and a few logical functions such as OR and AND. Multiplication and division are not provided on most micro- and mini-computers.

Associated with the ALU is a block labelled Registers (sometimes the term Accumulators is used). These are a small set of pigeon-holes each of which can hold one number. In *Fig. 1.2* four registers have been drawn, denoted A, B, C, D. Most microcomputers have more than this. Registers hold temporary data used in operations with the ALU. Typical instructions that the computer could be called on to perform are:

> Fetch the number from store location 3220 to Register A
> Fetch the number from store location 1956 to Register B
> Add the numbers in register A and register B and put the result in register A
> Subtract the number in store location 4057 from the number in register A and put the result in register A.

Computer arithmetical instructions usually involve a register and either another register or a store location. The results of an arithmetical operation always go to a register.

Bulk storage is often required on a computer, and this is usually provided by some form of magnetic store system. Tape units are popular on large mainframe computers, but micro- and mini-computers usually use magnetic discs or even the humble domestic cassette recorder. All these storage methods correspond directly to the filing cabinet in *Fig. 1.1*.

All the equipment in *Fig. 1.2* is co-ordinated by the block labelled 'control' which performs the same function as the human in *Fig. 1.1*. It is instructive to look at the functions the control block must perform:

> a. It will get the next instruction out of the store.
> b. Since the instruction is held as a number, the control must decide what this instruction number means. This is known as decoding.

c. Most instructions will involve simple operations between input/output/registers/ALU and one store location, typical examples being those given earlier. The control must set up the routes through the internal wiring to bring numbers to the correct place at the correct time.

d. With the routes set up, the instruction is obeyed.

e. Control determines where to get its next instruction. Since most instructions are obeyed sequentially, it is simplest to put the next instruction at the next address in the store, so control simply needs to step on to the next location. Control can them move back to step a and start obeying the next instruction.

It may not be immediately apparent, but the operation falls into three stages. First the control accesses the store to get the instruction, which it decodes and sets up the route. These are steps a–c above, sometimes called the Instruction Stage. Secondly, the control causes the instruction to be obeyed at step d, which probably requires the control to access the store again to get, or place, data. This is called the Data Stage. Finally control sets itself up for the next instruction at step e. Since this involves stepping on to the next instruction it is sometimes called the Incrementing Stage.

These three stages, Instruction, Data, Increment, are the heart beats of a computer, and the whole operation is conducted by the control unit. (The terms Fetch, Execute, and Reset are also frequently used for the three stages, since the control Fetches the instruction, Executes it, and Resets its internal logic ready for the next instruction.)

Marvin, a simple computer

In order to see how the various parts of *Fig. 1.2* fit together, we shall describe a hypothetical computer called Marvin. This machine is simpler than any real machine, but performs in a similar manner to its larger brethren.

Marvin has the block diagram of *Fig. 1.4*, which is really *Fig. 1.2* with data routes drawn on and a little more detail added. Most people are aware that computers work in something mysterious called Binary. For simplicity, Marvin does not; he works in decimal like you or I. Fortunately Marvin is only a paper computer so we do not need at this stage to consider how his circuits are made.

Marvin has 100 store locations with addresses 0 to 99. Each location can hold one positive or negative number in the range 0 to 999. As mentioned earlier, instructions and data are held in an identical manner, and the store does not know the difference between them. If a negative number is used as an instruction the sign is ignored.

Associated with the store are two blocks AB and MB which are, respectively the address buffer and the memory buffer. The address buffer holds the address of the store location being used, and hence holds a number in the range 0 to 99. The memory buffer is used as a 'staging post' for data going into and out of the store. The memory buffer thus holds numbers in the range 0 to 999. The control also provides a read/write signal which tells the store whether to take data from a location and put it in the memory buffer (called reading) or to take data from the memory buffer and put it in a store location (called writing). When a number is read from a store location the location is not left empty, a copy of the number is left behind. When a number is written into a location the previous contents are overwritten.

For simplicity, Marvin has only one register, denoted by A, and a simple adder/subtractor unit. From the connections it will be seen that the adder/subtractor works on the contents of the memory buffer and register A, and puts the result into register A again.

Marvin has only one input (a typewriter keyboard), and one output (a printer). These connect to the memory buffer as shown. When instructed to input, the control takes a number from the keyboard and puts it into the memory buffer, and from there to a store location specified by the program. When instructed to print, the control takes a number from a specified store location to the memory buffer, and from there to the printer.

Before we can describe the rest of Marvin's architecture, we must first decide how to decode a number when it is used

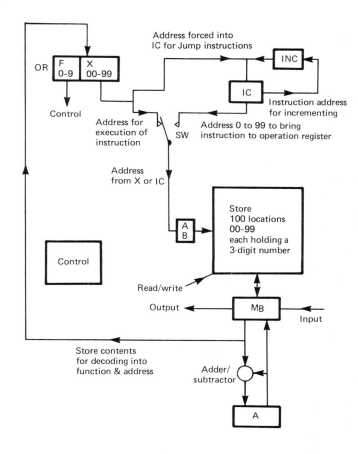

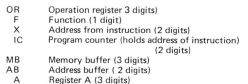

OR	Operation register 3 digits)
F	Function (1 digit)
X	Address from instruction (2 digits)
IC	Program counter (holds address of instruction)
	(2 digits)
MB	Memory buffer (3 digits)
AB	Address buffer (2 digits)
A	Register A (3 digits)

Figure 1.4. Architecture of Marvin

as an instruction. There are three digits to play with. Most instructions will involve a store location, so we will need to specify the location address somewhere in the instruction. There are 100 locations with addresses in the range 00 to 99, so we need two digits to specify the address. It would seem sensible to use the most significant digit to define what we are going to do, and the least significant two digits to define the store location involved. (*Fig. 1.5.*)

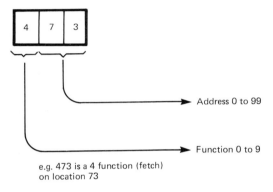

Address 0 to 99

Function 0 to 9

e.g. 473 is a 4 function (fetch)
on location 73

Figure 1.5. Marvin's instruction format

The number 578 is thus a 5 instruction (whatever that may be) on store location 78. We must now allocate our ten functions, 0 to 9.

Our first requirement is obviously getting data into the machine, so we will allocate 0 as input:

0XX input a number to store location XX.

The computer will output a ? on the printer and wait for the operator to type in a number. The number is then transferred to the specified location.

Obviously the next requirement is output. We will use function 1 for this and define:

1XX take the number in store location XX and print it on the printer

12

We will deal with the arithmetical instructions next:

2XX add the contents of store location XX to the contents of register A, and put the result in register A

3XX subtract the contents of store location XX from the contents of Register A, and put the result in register A

When the result is put into register A, the previous contents are overwritten. The store location contents are unaffected.

The next two instructions are needed to move numbers between the store and register A:

4XX fetch the contents of store location XX to register A

5XX store the contents of register A in store location XX

In both cases the original contents of the destination are overwritten and the contents of the source are unaltered. Let us assume we have 123 in store location 67 and 456 in register A. If we performed instruction 467 we would still have 123 in store location 67 and 123 in register A. If we started with these same numbers in location 67 and register A, and performed instruction 567 we would have 456 in location 67 and 456 remaining in register A.

In the absence of any instruction to the contrary, a computer will assume that the first instruction is held at location 0, and will obey the instructions in successive store locations one at a time. With the six instructions we have defined so far we can write a simple program to input two numbers, add them together and print the result.

Location	Contents	Meaning
0	099	Input first number to location 99
1	098	Input second number to location 98
2	499	Fetch first number to register A
3	298	Add second number
4	597	Put result in location 97
5	197	Print result

As yet we cannot stop the machine, so after obeying our instructions the control would step on to location 6 and obey the number held there, followed by location 7, and so on.

A computer that simply starts at location 0 and works its way up the store is little more than a glorified calculator. The

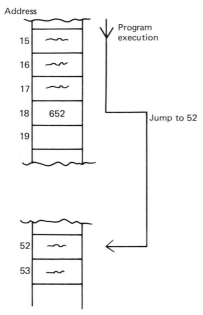

Figure 1.6. The jump instruction

next three instructions allow the computer to jump around the store. The first of these is called the unconditional jump, defined as:

> 6XX the next instruction is at location XX

Having obeyed the instruction in XX, the computer follows it with XX + 1, XX + 2 as shown on *Fig. 1.6.*

If we take our simple addition program above, and put 600 in location 6, the computer would jump back to location 0 and go round and round the instructions.

The next two instructions are called conditional jumps, and these allow the computer to choose alternative routes according to conditions. Both conditonal jumps test the condition of register A, and are known as jump negative and jump zero:

> 7XX the next instruction is at location XX if the register A is negative

> 8XX the next instruction is at location XX if the register A is zero

If the condition is met, the instruction behaves as the jump instruction. If the condition is not met, the instruction is ignored.

The tenth, and final instruction is simple:

> 9XX STOP. The value of XX is irrelevant.

When we modified our simple addition program by adding a jump instruction, we left it going round a loop. With a conditional jump and the stop instruction the operator can bring it out of the loop by putting zero in when asked for his two numbers:

Location	Contents	Meaning
0	099	Input first number to location 99
1	098	Input second number to location 98
2	499	Fetch first number to register A
3	298	Add second number
4	597	Store result in location 97
5	197	Print result
6	808	Jump to location 8 if register A is zero
7	600	Jump back for another go
8	900	STOP

At location 6 we look at the result of the addition. If we have added two zeros, the result will be zero and we will go to the stop instruction at location 8. If the result is not zero we go to the next instruction at location 7 which is a jump instruction back to the start of the program. Remembering that the computer prompts the operator with ?, Marvin would run this program as below:

```
GO
?   12      ?   3       15
?   123     ?   56      179
?   0       ?   5       5
?   0       ?   0       0        Halted
```

Programming in this manner is known as machine-code programming, and a few points should be apparent. Firstly, it is very tedious since each and every step has to be written. Secondly, since any number is a valid instruction, one wrong instruction can easily cause the program to go off the rails, probably destroying the correct parts of the program as it does so. Finally, a machine-code program consisting of a lot of numbers is almost incomprehensible without comments. In later chapters we will discuss assembler languages and high-level languages which overcome these problems.

Before examining Marvin's architecture further here is a program showing how to multiply two numbers:

Location	Contents	Meaning
0	099	Input first number to location 99
1	098	Input second number to location 98
2	414	Bring zero to register A
3	597	Store register A in partial result (location 97)
4	299	Add first number
5	597	Store register A in partial result
6	498	Fetch contents of location 98

Location	Contents	Meaning
7	315	Subtract one
8	812	If register A is zero, go to print out
9	598	Store register A in location 98
10	497	Bring partial result to register A
11	604	Jump back
12	197	Print result
13	900	Stop
14	000	Zero
15	001	One

It will be left as an exercise for the reader to follow it through, but a few useful hints will be given. It works by successive addition, so that if we multiplied 7 by 13 it would add up 7 thirteen times (a very long-winded way!). The two numbers are held in locations 99 and 98. The number in 99 is added up the number of times held in 98, so if you multiply 3 by 256, say, the program will work quicker with 256 in location 99 and 3 in location 98. (Think about it!) Location 97 is used to hold the running total. Locations 14 and 15 are not instructions, they are numbers zero and one respectively. (Although 000 and 001 are legitimate instructions, and would be obeyed if the computer encountered them in error because, say, the programmer had forgotten the Stop instruction at location 13.)

Now the rest of Marvin's architecture: OR stands for Operation Register, and is used to hold the three-digit number corresponding to the current instructions. This is split into a two-digit block X for the address used by the instruction and a single digit F which defines the instruction. When the computer is obeying an instruction the control decodes F to set up the route, and uses X to address the store. The desired instruction can then be performed.

The block IC (for 'instruction counter') holds the address of the current instruction, and is used to address the store during the instruction part of the operation. The address buffer (AB) is thus connected to either IC (during the instruction stage) or X (during the data stage) by an electronic changeover switch SW.

For instruction functions 0 to 5, IC is simply stepped on to the next location when the instruction is completed. This is performed by the block INC which adds one to the contents of IC.

For instruction function 6 (jump) IC needs to take the next instruction address from X (remember the operation of the jump instruction).

The conditional jumps (functions 7 and 8) simply set the instruction counter to the X value if the condition is met. If the condition is not met, IC is loaded from INC in the normal manner.

We have deliberately not discussed Marvin's physical construction; the next section and the rest of the book will describe microcomputer circuits. There are also several practical points that may have occurred to the reader, such as how we load a program in the first place, and what an operator's panel looks like. Such points will also be covered later when we look at real machines.

1, 10 buckle my shoe

As most people are aware, computers operate in something called Binary, and this has probably been responsible for most of the mystique surrounding the machines. In practice, computers operate in binary (with a small b to show its unimportance!) for reasons of simple economics, and the binary number system is so simple that children at junior school level (with no preconceived notions on numbers) can easily grasp it. Usually, the binary system is described in a formal textbook manner. This section describes the reasons for its use in computing in a more intuitive manner. To do this we will try to design some of Marvin's circuits.

Marvin works by manipulating three-digit decimal numbers, so we will need to find some way of representing, and storing, numbers from 0 to 999 electronically.

For practical reasons we can rule out analog systems, which represent the digits 0 to 9 by, say, 0 to 9 volts in 1 volt steps. At each block in *Fig. 1.4* we would have three wires (one for each decade) and 30 level detectors! Apart from being very expensive in circuitry, the setting of all the level detectors would be a maintenance engineer's nightmare. The circuits would also be prone to error as it would be easy to have, say, a high 7 (e.g. 7.2 volts) with a bit of noise (e.g. 0.5 volts spike) being recognized as an 8 by an 8V detector reading slightly low.

The most reliable circuits are those with only two states, on and off. Common examples are simple switches and relays. Similarly, logic circuits are designed around two, and only two, voltages called '1' and '0'. A common set of circuits called TTL uses 3.5V for 1 and 0V for 0. Detailed knowledge of logic circuits is not essential to understand this book, but a brief introduction to logic circuits is given in the companion books 'Beginner's Guide to Computers' and 'Beginner's Guide to Integrated Circuits'.

Given the 1 and 0 approach, how can we code 0 to 999 with 1s and 0s? The obvious method would be to use 10 wires for each decade and energise one wire to represent the number. The blocks of *Fig. 1.4* would be interconnected by 30-way ribbon cables, and the switch SW would be a 30-way changeover switch. Each block would contain 30 circuits.

This design could certainly be made to work, but it is by no means the most economical circuit possible. Considerable savings can be made by realising that all the numbers from 0 to 9 can be represented by combinations of 1, 2, 4, and 8:

0	none
1	1
2	2
3	2,1
4	4
5	4,1
6	4,2
7	4,2,1
8	8
9	8,1

We can thus represent the numbers from 0 to 9 by four wires representing 8, 4, 2, and 1 and putting a 1 on the wires that give the required number. To cover the three decades 0 to 999 we will need 12-way ribbon cables, and 12 circuits at each block or switch. This is known as BCD (for binary coded decimal) and is used in simple calculators. It is not, however, the most economical design.

A few minutes work with a pencil and paper will demonstrate that all numbers from 0 to 1023 can be represented by combinations of:

1, 2, 4, 8, 16, 32, 64, 128, 256, 512

999, for example, can be made up of:

512 + 256 + 128 + 64 + 32 + 4 + 2 + 1

This coding would allow Marvin to be built around 10-way ribbon cables and blocks of ten circuits. The saving over BCD is small for three decades, but increases dramatically for larger numbers. Sixteen lines in BCD can represent 0 to 9999. Sixteen lines used as multiples of two can represent 0 to 65 536.

Using multiples of two to represent numbers is, quite simply, the binary system and it can be shown to be the most economical manner in which a computer can be constructed. In addition, all the circuits of the various blocks of *Fig. 1.4* (such as the adder) are much simpler in binary than in BCD.

Using binary to build a computer simplifies the design and reduces the cost and complexity at the expense of some slight inconvenience to the user. This inconvenience will be minimal providing the inputs and outputs are in decimal or some other recognisable form.

Marvin in binary
Constructing Marvin in binary will make little, if any, difference to the block diagram of *Fig. 1.2* but will cause us to rethink the way we code instructions. A common standard is to use 16 binary lines to represent numbers, so the contents of a store could look like this:

1101110011010110

which means little to anyone! Chapter 3 will look at short-hand ways of representing binary numbers so humans can deal with them.

Each power of 2 (i.e. each line) is called a bit (from BInary digiT), so with 16 lines we have a 16-bit word. With 16 bits we can represent numbers from 0 to 65 536. It is not really feasible to split up the instruction between function and address in a decimal fashion as we did on *Fig. 1.5*. A more sensible manner would be to allocate, say, the top four bits to the function and the bottom 12 bits to the address as shown in *Fig. 1.7*.

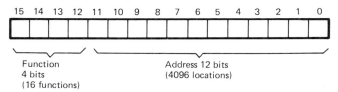

| 15 | 14 | 13 | 12 | 11 | 10 | 9 | 8 | 7 | 6 | 5 | 4 | 3 | 2 | 1 | 0 |

Function
4 bits
(16 functions)

Address 12 bits
(4096 locations)

Figure 1.7. A binary computer word

The four function bits can represent 0000 to 1111, or 0 to 15 in decimal. We thus have 16 function codes available (the reader might like to think how he would allocate the six additional codes; in Chapter 3 we will see what instructions are available on real machines).

The twelve function bits can represent 0 to 4095 in decimal. We can thus address 4096 store locations (called 4K in the jargon). Binary addressing leads to apparently peculiar store sizes such as:

10 bits – 1024, called 1K
12 bits – 4096, called 4K
13 bits – 8192, called 8K
14 bits – 16384, called 16K
15 bits – 32768, called 32K
16 bits – 65536, called 64K

Note that a 64K store has actually over 65 000 locations. The use of K in computing is not the strict electronic definition of 1000.

Conclusion

Marvin, even in his 16-bit binary form, is a very simple machine. Every computer ever built, however, has the same basic block diagram and the same philosophy. The only differences among computers are their sizes, the range of instructions, the types of peripheral devices added to the machines and the ways in which the blocks in *Fig. 1.2* are implemented by the electronics.

Of necessity, the introduction to computers in this chapter has been rather brief. Readers requiring more detail on computers in general are referred to the companion book 'Beginner's Guide to Computers'.

2

The microcomputer

Integrated circuits

One of the more common confusions brought about by the use of the words 'chip' and 'microchip' is the belief that the words 'integrated circuit' and 'microprocessor' describe the same device. Like most microprocessor myths and fallacies this confusion has been brought about by garbled media reports. Before we describe a microprocessor chip, we first need to know what an integrated circuit is.

The basis of all modern electronics is the transistor. A transistor is formed by the twin processes of etching and addition of carefully controlled impurities to very small slices of silicon or germanium. The actual slice of silicon or germanium is typically 1 mm square, and the physical size of a transistor case is determined solely by the need to handle the device and dissipate any heat generated internally.

From the beginning of transistor manufacture it was obvious that several transistors and resistors could be manufactured on one slice, and connected together by etched aluminium wires, but the theory took several years to turn into practice. The etching of the silicon (or germanium) slices is done by photographic methods similar to the developing of a normal film, but the extremely small sizes of the slices needed very fine grain film and very precise positioning of the negatives.

The second problem was yield. The slices need to be very pure, but total purity can never be attained. It was found that as more devices were packed on to a slice, the probability of encountering a flaw rose, and the yield from the production line fell. Before the circuit on a chip could be realised, therefore, improvements had to be made in the photographic techniques and the quality of the basic chip material.

There are several reasons why the development of circuits on a chip, or integrated circuits as they became known, was important. In the manufacture of any electronic equipment, the design costs can be spread out over all the items sold. The major cost of any electronic item therefore is usually the labour costs of assembly, and as circuits using integrated circuits are easier to assemble there are considerable cost savings to be made. This is well demonstrated by the way items such as calculators and televisions have fallen in price despite inflation.

Integrated circuits also lead to increased reliability. In most circuits the common failures are actually mechanical in origin; faults such as plugs and sockets, bad soldering and cracks in printed circuit board tracks. By reducing the number of interconnections, the overall reliability is improved. The early work on integrated circuits was, in fact, financed largely by military funds to provide high reliability electronics for the hostile environments of rockets and satellites.

Finally the small size of the integrated circuit allows circuits to operate at higher speed. It is not generally appreciated that in many circuits, the operating speed is limited by the time taken for signals to pass down the interconnecting wires. If the circuit can be made physically smaller it can therefore be made faster.

The first integrated circuits appeared commercially in the early 1960s, and became more complex as techniques improved. The early chips were simple logic gates but medium scale integration (MSI) soon brought counter and shift register functions and large scale integration (LSI) provided more complex functions such as calculators and digital watches.

By 1970, manufacturers were able to produce complex LSI chips, but an interesting economic effect occurred. The design and tooling costs of an i.c.p. are considerable, but this is offset by the very large sales. The sheer volume of production allows a 7400 quad NAND integrated circuit to sell for less than the cost of a single transistor. As chips became more complicated, however, they became more specialised and the market became smaller. Semiconductor manufacturers were reaching the point where they could manufacture very complex LSI chips, but the price would be prohibitively high.

Enter the microprocessor

The microprocessor is often thought to be a very modern device, but the first microprocessor chip widely offered for sale was probably the Intel 4040 in 1970. Intel had reached the

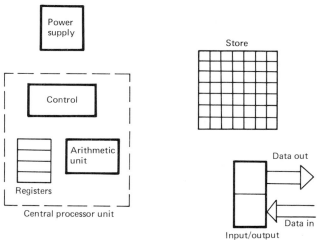

Figure 2.1. Elements of a microcomputer

stage outlined above and were looking for markets for LSI chips.

In *Fig. 2.1* we have the now-familiar computer block diagram. The dotted box in older machines was known as the Central Processor Unit, or CPU. The Intel engineers realised

25

that to manufacture a computer on a chip was not really feasible (or desirable, since each application is different), but the CPU could easily be made with LSI. There is very little variation in CPU design, so a CPU chip could be used to build all types of computers from a small washing machine programmer to a large commercial computer. The CPU thus met the criterion for volume sales.

It cannot be emphasised too strongly that a microprocessor in NOT a computer. To construct a working computer all the additional components shown on *Fig. 2.1* are needed. The microprocessor is thus only a small portion of the machine. When all the additional components are added we have a working machine called a microcomputer.

The microprocessor revealed
A typical microprocessor will be a 40-pin integrated circuit package (i.c.p.) similar to *Fig. 2.2*, containing the elements of

Figure 2.2. A DIL chip

the CPU of a computer. Inside the microprocessor there will be:

    i. Registers.
   ii. Instruction counter.
  iii. Arithmetic and logic unit (ALU).
  iv. Instruction decode, control and timing.

The microprocessor will provide signals to the other elements of *Fig. 2.1*. These signals are conveyed on cables known as highways:

26

i. Addresses for the store and input/output unit.
ii. Data to the store and output unit.
iii. Data from the store and input unit.
iv. Control signals such as input/output, read/write, and timing pulses.

Signals i. and iv. are always *from* the microprocessor. The data signals flow in two directions, and are implemented by means of a single bidirectional data highway, rather than by two separate data highways. Signals are connected on to the highway by logic elements known as TriState gates. These have outputs which can be turned to a high-impedance (floating) state when not in use, as shown in *Fig. 2.3.*

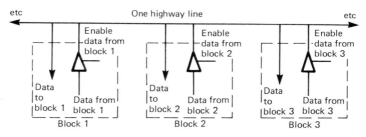

Figure 2.3. The TriState highway

All microprocessors work in binary, and most use an eight-bit word called a Byte. Most microprocessors can address up to 64K of store, which requires 16 bits. The programming of a microprocessor is thus somewhat more involved than the direct function/address method used by Marvin in the previous chapter. The eight-bit word of the microprocessor is a real handicap compared with the 16-bit word used by minicomputers. The next generation of 16-bit microprocessors will, however, produce microcomputers as powerful as today's minicomputers. In Chapter 3 the programming of the microprocessor will be described, and how the difficulty of addressing 64K of store with an eight-bit word is overcome.

A typical microprocessor therefore communicates with the rest of the computer via a 16-bit address highway, an eight-bit bidirectional data highway and a few control lines. The highway concept is very useful, as it allows easy expansion of the system at some future date. Quite often the word 'bus' (short for busbar) is used instead of highway.

A typical microprocessor contains elements like those shown in *Fig. 2.4*. Each manufacturer's microprocessor differs in detail, but most have the features described below.

Data to and from the store and I/O is carried on the eight-bit data highway and connects to the microprocessor via the data buffer. This is simply a two-way TriState buffer to control the direction of the data flow. The data buffer connects to an internal eight-bit data bus.

Instructions are read into the instruction buffer from the data highway and are decoded by the control logic as described previously. In Chapter 3 how a microprocessor can address a 64K store will be explained, but at this stage simply note that the instruction buffer will need to hold more than eight bits.

The simple computer, Marvin, had a single register/accumulator. Microprocessors have several registers for increased versatility; our example has eight, identified by the letters A, B, C, D, E, F, H, L.

B, C, D, E, H and L are simple eight-bit (one word) stores used to hold data required in a hurry. By computer standards, store read/writes are slow operations, but data transfers within a microprocessor i.c.p. are very fast. The sensible use of the internal registers greatly reduces program execution times, apart from giving the programmer more flexibility.

Registers A and F are special-purpose eight-bit registers. A is the accumulator, and is used to hold the results of all arithmetical operations in the ALU. Registers B, C, D, E, H and L can be used as sources of data for the ALU, but all results go to A. This restriction arises primarily from the complexity of instruction coding that would be needed if the destination of an ALU result could be specified. In practice

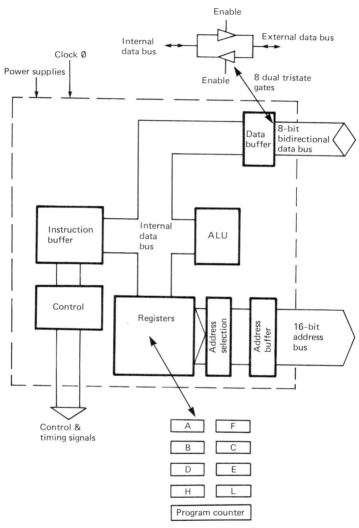

Figure 2.4. A typical microprocessor

29

little inconvenience is caused because data transfer can take place between all internal registers with single instructions.

Register F is known as the flag register. Programmers often need to know if certain events have occurred in arithmetical operations. Typical of these events are overflow (the result has gone over eight bits), underflow (the result has gone negative), and zero result. The eight bits of the flag register are set by the ALU logic. The actual allocation of the bits in the flag register varies considerably from manufacturer to manufacturer. Those provided by the Z-80 are typical:

Bit	Symbol	Operation
0	C	Carry produced from most significant bit
1	N	Last operation was a subtraction
2	P	Parity (holds parity of result)
3	–	Not used
4	H	Half carry occurred (from bit 3 to bit 4 of A)
5	–	Not used
6	Z	Zero result
7	S	Sign of result

The flag register can be used to give many forms of conditional jump (Marvin only had jump zero and jump positive). The contents of the flag register can be transferred freely to any other register for examination.

The final register is the instruction counter (sometimes called the program counter) which holds the address of the current instruction. With 64K locations the instruction counter will hold a 16-bit word. Associated with the instruction counter is the incrementing logic for normal sequential operation and the jump logic to obtain a new address from the instruction buffer.

The six registers B, C, D, E, H, L are eight-bit registers, but logic is provided to enable them to be linked into three 16-bit registers denoted BC, DE, HL. The use of this feature will be described later.

The microprocessor addresses 64K of store via a 16-bit address highway. This address can be obtained from the instruction counter, the instruction buffer or the register pairs BC, DE, HL dependent on the operation being performed. The address source is selected by the address selection logic under the direction of the control logic.

The control logic also supplies the external control signals. These include the store read/write controls, input/output selection and sundry timing signals and strobes. A typical microprocessor will have about twelve signals on the control highway.

To obtain timing signals some form of 'conductor' is needed and this is provided by an external oscillator. The oscillator is known as the clock, and is denoted by the Greek letter φ. Most microprocessors work with clock frequencies between 1 and 4 MHz. Each instruction takes several clock pulses to complete, so a 1 MHz clock does not mean the microprocessor will obey one million instructions per second.

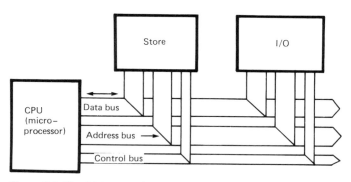

Figure 2.5. The highways of a microcomputer

We can now draw a block diagram of a typical microcomputer system, which is the surprisingly simple *Fig. 2.5*. It consists of the microprocessor and its clock generator, some form of store and the I/0 units, all interconnected by the three highways: eight-bit data, 16-bit address and the control signals.

Storage systems

All computer systems, however humble, need some form of
storage to hold both the data being processed and the
instructions controlling the computer. In earlier sections it
was described how both instructions and data were held in
the form of binary numbers stored in 'pigeon-holes', each
pigeon-hole being identified by a unique address. Most
microprocessors work with an eight-bit word, and anything
from a few hundred store locations up to large systems with
over 64 000 locations. All storage systems, however, are
designed simply to store bits.

Fig. 2.6a shows one possible circuit for storing and reading
one bit. Eight identical circuits are needed to store an

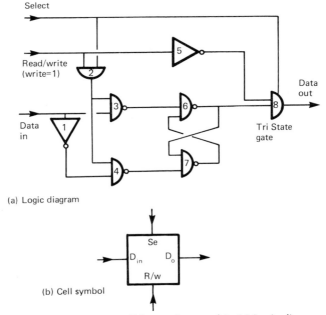

(a) Logic diagram

(b) Cell symbol

Figure 2.6. A memory cell for storing one bit. (a) Logic diagram.
(b) Cell symbol

eight-bit word. The circuit in *Fig. 2.6a* is known as a memory cell, and has four connections to the outside world.

The select line 'enables' the cell (explained later), and is at a 1 when the computer calls for the particular address of which this cell forms one part. With the read/write line at a 1 data is written into the storage flip-flop constructed from gates 6 and 7, via gates 3 and 4. With the read/write line at a 0, data is read via the TriState gate 8 to the outside world. The memory cell can therefore be represented by the block diagram of *Fig. 2.6b*.

To store one word eight memory cells are needed and are connected as shown in *Fig. 2.7*. The read/write lines and the select lines will be commoned, and there will be eight data in lines and eight data out lines.

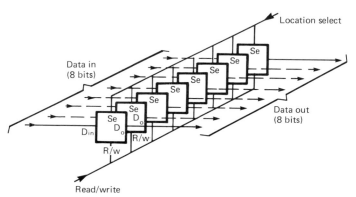

Figure 2.7. A store location

The method of organising several store locations similar to *Fig. 2.7* into a storage system for a computer must now be decided. *Fig. 2.5* shows that the store connects to the computer via a 16-bit address highway, and an eight-bit data highway. The first requirement, therefore, is to decode the 16-bit address to provide the select lines for *Fig. 2.7*.

Here a small simplification, purely to aid the clarity of the drawings is introduced. A 16-bit address highway can address over 64 000 locations. Drawings of a 64K storage system

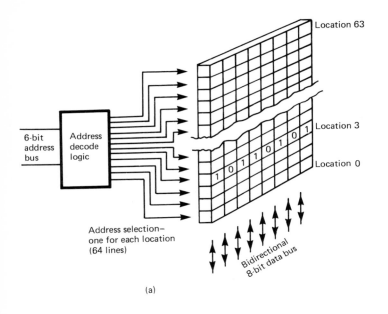

(a)

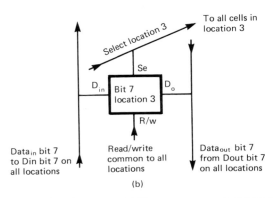

(b)

Figure 2.8. A 64-location store. (a) Store arrangement. (b) One cell in the store

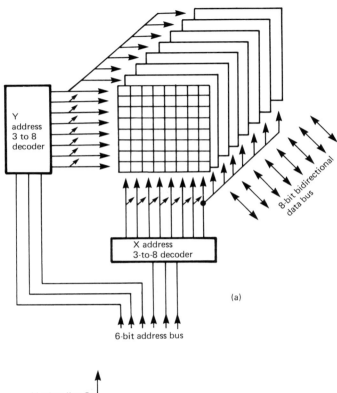

(a)

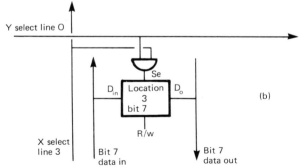

(b)

Figure 2.9. X–Y addressed store. (a) Store organisation. (b) One cell

35

would be impossibly complex, so a very simple store with just 64 locations will be described. This works in an identical manner to its larger brethren, but is easier to draw!

A 64-location store requires six bits to address it, so conceptually it looks rather like the tower block of *Fig. 2.8a*. The six address lines are decoded into 64 select lines (from address 0 to address 63), which connect to all the cells in one location. The data in and data out lines connect to ALL the data in and data out connections for that bit. The read/write line links ALL the read/write connections in the memory. *Fig. 2.6b* summarises the connections to one of the cells. All other cells are similar. In the 64-location memory there will be 64 × 8 (512) storage cells all connected in a similar manner.

Although the user can consider all memories arranged as a tower block, the design of larger memories presents the semiconductor manufacturers with the problem of decoding 16 bits into 65 536 select lines. This is overcome by the use of column and row addressing (called X,Y addressing). Instead of arranging a column of locations, the designer uses a square. The 64 locations in the example could be arranged as planes of 8 × 8 cells as shown on *Fig. 2.9a*. To store eight-bit words eight planes are needed.

The six-bit address is now split into a three-bit column address and a three-bit row address, to give eight row select lines and eight column select lines. Each cell is connected to one row and one column line to select the cell. As before, all the data in lines and all the data out lines are paralleled on one plane, and the read/write line is commoned on all planes.

The saving on a 64-location store is minimal, but the saving on larger stores is considerable. A 16K memory (with 16 384 locations) will be organised in 128 × 128 planes. Two 7-bit to 128 decoders are obviously far simpler to design than one 14-bit to 16 384 decoder! The user, however, need not really consider how the 16K memory is organised. To him, it appears as a tower block.

Integrated circuit stores are designed to represent one plane of *Fig. 2.9a* (or one column of *Fig. 2.8a* if the reader

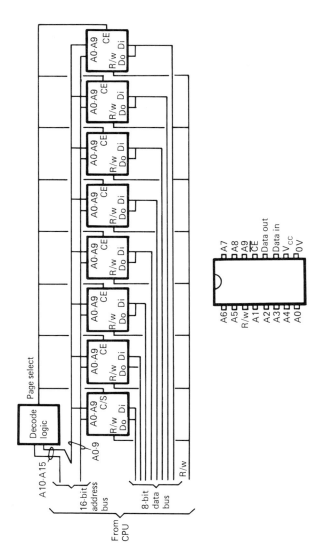

Figure 2.10. Organisation of 1K store

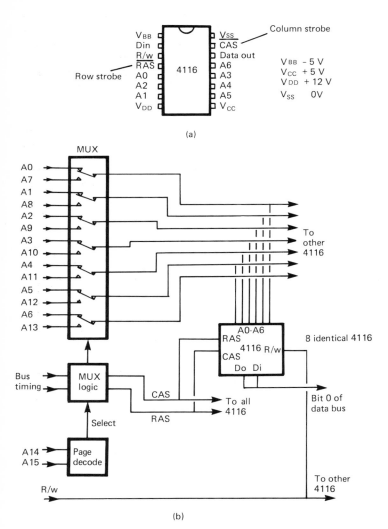

Figure 2.11. The 4116 dynamic RAM. (a) The 4116 pin arrangement. (b) Row/column decode

prefers to think in terms of tower blocks). The 2102 i.c.p. is a 1K store, described as a 1K × 1-bit memory since it contains 1024 memory cells. To store 1024 eight bit words would need eight identical 2102 i.c.p.s connected as in *Fig. 2.10*.

The 2102 store has all ten address lines brought out. In *Fig. 2.11a* is the popular 4116 16K × 1-bit store. It will be noted that only seven address lines are given, but fourteen lines are needed to address 16K. The designers of the memory i.c.p. had to work within the constraints of a 16 pin i.c.p., and there are simply not enough pins to allow all address lines to be brought out.

The solution lies in the two strobe lines, Row Strobe and Column Strobe. The row address and column address are loaded separately on the same seven address lines. This is accomplished by the simple logic of *Fig. 2.11b*. The read/write and data lines operate as before.

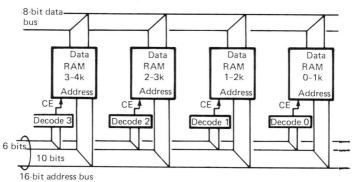

Figure 2.12. Use of 'enable' pins to select store blocks

The 4116 is a dynamic RAM, and the use of the row address strobe simplifies refreshing. The meaning of 'dynamic' and 'refreshing' is described in the following section on store terminology.

Most i.c.p. memories have a pin labelled CE for 'chip enable'. This allows the memory to be placed anywhere within the 64K address range of the highway. In *Fig. 2.12* we have four blocks of 1K memory (each block being eight i.c.p.s similar to *Fig. 2.10*). These blocks use the bottom ten bits of the address highway on their address lines. Some simple decoding logic is connected to the remaining six bits, and provides outputs for '0', '1', '2' and '3'. Block 1 is enabled for addresses 0 to 1023, block 2 for addresses 1024 to 2047 and so on.

By the use of decoding logic and the chip enable pins, 64K store can be made up from four 16K blocks, eight 8K blocks, sixteen 4K blocks or any combination thereof. Obviously all 64K does not have to be used, and the computer will operate quite happily with smaller stores providing the user never tries to access non-existent locations!

Occasionally the term 'core' is used to describe a computer store. This is a hangover from older computer systems and the large mainframe computers which use small magnetic cores for storage cells. These are fast, and keep their contents during a power failure. They are, however, bulky and need considerable supply currents to operate. Their use is almost unknown in microcomputers, but from time to time engineers refer to the store as 'the core'. The operation of core stores is described in 'Beginner's Guide to Computers'.

Store terminology

The first pair of terms encountered is 'volatile' and 'non-volatile'. This determines whether or not the store contents (and hence the program and data) are lost if the power is turned off. A non-volatile store will keep its contents through a power failure, a volatile store will lose its contents.

Magnetic storage systems (magnetic cores, discs, drums and tapes) are non-volatile. All common semiconductor stores are inherently volatile, but this is not the disadvantage it might seem. The current drawn by a semiconductor store is minimal, and it is quite feasible to power a store and any ancillary logic by small batteries. These are known as 'battery-supported stores', and a typical example is shown in *Fig. 2.13*. This is a store board from an industrial control computer, which will hold its contents for about four weeks in the absence of power. The battery is normally trickle-charged from the computer power supply. Provision is made for running the board on a 9 V dry cell should the on-board rechargeable battery need replacement. A recent innovation is a conventional store i.c.p. (MK48Z02) with integral battery which obviates the need for a separate battery.

The second pair of terms used to describe stores are 'static' and 'dynamic'. These refer only to semiconductor stores, and describe the manner in which the storage cell of *Fig. 2.6* is achieved. A static cell is simplest, and will be described first.

Figure 2.13. A battery-supported RAM

The actual storage in a static cell will be some form of cross-coupled FET (Field Effect Transistor) flip-flop similar to *Fig. 2.14a*. This works in a very simple manner, since if TR1 is on, TR2 will be off and vice versa. Data is forced in via TR2 and TR4 and can be read on D out. The simple static store, however, suffers from the disadvantage that it requires (in electronic terms) a large supply current.

In *Fig. 2.14b* the storage cell is redrawn with row select transistors TR5, TR6 and capacitors C1, C2 added. If the cell is turned off by de-selecting the row, capacitors C1 and C2 will maintain the voltages on TR1, TR2. On reselecting the row, the memory cell will take up its previous state again.

Obviously, C1 and C2 do not hold the data for long enough to make the store non-volatile, but they do allow considerable power savings to be made by putting cells into a dormant state when not in use. The small capacitors are implemented by the inherent inter-junction capacitance of the transistors.

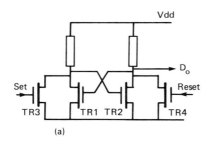

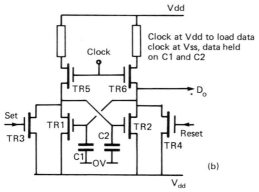

Figure 2.14. Static and dynamic memories. (a) Static memory cell. (b) Dynamic memory cell

A store using this technique to conserve power is known as a dynamic store. The data has to be continually preserved by clocking the row select lines in sequence when the store is not in use. This is known as 'refreshing', and needs to be done every 2 ms (which is a long time for a computer).

Refreshing is done automatically by some microprocessors, but can also be achieved by a simple counter since all that is needed is the clocking of eight bits of the address highway. If the store is to be battery-supported, the refresh logic must also be supported.

A major constraint on the operating speed of any computer is the time taken to put data into and out of the store. This is defined as the 'store cycle time' which is roughly the time taken to address the store and read, or write, data. An average value for the cycle time of a semiconductor store is 200 ns. Sometimes the term 'access time' is used.

The final term is the one that seems to cause most confusion; RAM, or Random Access Memory. Consider a computer where the numbers in a store are recorded in some form on a magnetic tape. To write or read data, the computer would have to spool the tape to the required spot on the tape. The cycle time is not constant and depends on the last store location used and the next location required.

In the semiconductor store, however, the cycle time does not depend on the last store location used, and that, simply, is all Random Access Memory means. Every store location can be accessed in any order with the same cycle time. Stores such as disc and tapes are 'serially accessed stores'.

Program storage
Once all the faults have been removed from a program, the instructions will probably not need to be changed again. If the program is unlikely to be changed, it is unnecessary (and potentially hazardous) to hold it in normal read/write memory. The program will be far more secure if it can be stored in store locations which can be read from, but not written to. Such a store is called a ROM or Read Only Memory.

A ROM looks, to the computer, like any other store system described earlier; it shares the same address data and control highway as the rest of the store. The only difference is that its contents are 'built-in' at the manufacturing stage and cannot be altered by the computer.

Mask-programmed ROMs are used where many identical ROMs are needed (e.g. monitors, assemblers, computer toys, cash registers, consumer goods). The store contents are set up by superimposing a specially designed aluminium grid on to a universal storage i.c.p. chip. The grid (known as a mask) is designed by the semiconductor manufacturer for the specific program. This technique is prohibitively expensive for a few ROMs, but is by far the cheapest method for production line quantities.

Programmable ROMs (or PROMs) are formed by destroying selected small fusible links inside an i.c.p. These tiny fuses are blown by selecting the required address and pulsing a large current. PROMs can be manufactured in small quantities quite cheaply, and a PROM blaster can be found in most electronic laboratories.

Once programmed, a PROM or mask-programmed ROM cannot be changed. A type of ROM known as an Erasable Programmable Read Only Memory (or EPROM) allows the user (but not the computer) to change the contents. The data is held on super-low-leakage capacitors on a slice. Loading the store causes selected capacitors to be charged which can then be read in the normal manner. The computer cannot write to these capacitors, and the low leakage current means the charge can be held for years.

The EPROM is erased by exposure to ultraviolet light through a quartz window in the top of the i.c.p. This

Figure 2.15. Photograph of EPROM

44

discharges the capacitors, leaving the memory blank and ready for re-writing. An EPROM is shown in *Fig. 2.15*. EPROMs are loaded by a Prom Programmer and erased by a UV light in a safety case. Users of EPROMs should be aware of the health hazards of UV light sources and take suitable precautions.

Bulk storage
In *Fig. 1.1* a 'filing cabinet' was shown as part of a computer. This is called the backing store, and is used to hold complete programs and bulk data. Most common bulk storage systems are based on magnetic discs, drums or tapes.

Although backing stores are an essential part of a large computer system, they are really peripheral devices and are dealt with further in Chapter 4.

Inputs and outputs

Input/output is dealt with in detail in Chapters 4 and 5 but the basic philosophy is described below. All input and output devices are connected to the address, data and control highways in a similar manner to the store (see *Fig. 2.16*).

Every input/output device has an address. The printer could have, say, address 3; a tape reader address 82 and a row of eight push-buttons address 257. To avoid confusion with computer addresses, the term 'port' is used. The tape reader above would be said to be connected to port 82.

The computer can then obey instructions such as:
    Put the data from register A to port 3
    Get the data from port 257 and put it in register B

Microprocessors deal with I/O port addresses in different ways. Some (such as the Motorola 6800) deal with both store and port addresses in the same manner, and it is not possible to have a port and store location with the same address. Some (such as the Z-80) have separate read/write and input/output control lines which allow the store and I/O to share addresses.

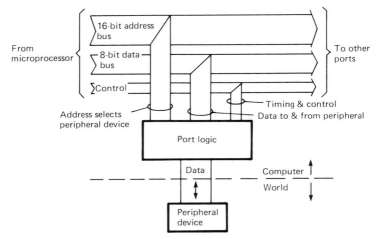

Figure 2.16. Connection of peripherals

The major problem with I/O is the vast disparity of speed between all I/O devices and the computer. Great care needs to be taken in the design of the I/O to computer interface to stop the slow I/O devices affecting the operating speed of the computer. These techniques are described further in Chapter 4.

Power supplies

An often overlooked item is the power supply, which often forms a significant part of the computer hardware costs. In an industrial control computer the power supply can occupy about one-third of the rack space and cost as much as a RAM card.

Computer power supplies are designed to very tight specifications. Most small microcomputers will require a +5 volt logic supply at 3 amps, +12 V supply (for the RAM) at about 0.25 amps, and a −5 volt supply (for the RAM and some microprocessors) at about 0.1 amps. These supplies must be maintained to within ±0.25 volts.

46

In addition, these supplies must be turned on, and off, in a specified sequence. The appearance of the + 5 volt supply without the + 12 volt supply will be followed by the death of the store. Similarly, the failure of the 12 volt supply must cause an automatic shutdown of the 5 volt supply.

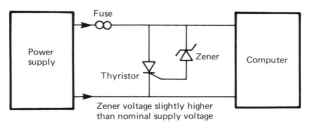

Figure 2.17. Crowbar trip circuit for overvoltage protection

Damage can also be caused by a supply going above its nominal voltage. Commercial supplies incorporate crowbar trips to short out a supply which starts to go overvoltage. These are usually based on the zener diode/thyristor circuit of *Fig. 2.17.* When a crowbar trip operates the whole supply shuts down. An industrial supply often incorporates logic

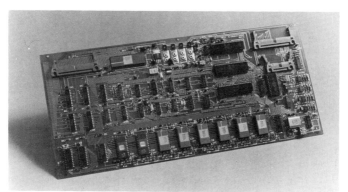

Figure 2.18. A complete control computer with CPU, RAM, ROM, Serial and Parallel I/O. (Photo: Scomagg Ltd)

which tests the protection circuits before applying power to the computer.

A common problem with computer power supplies is mains-borne noise. Equipment such as thyristor drives, light dimmers, relays and motors generate noise spikes which can write all sorts of peculiar data into RAMs. A good power supply will incorporate very efficient mains filters.

From the above it will be gathered that the design of computer power supplies is best left to the professionals.

3

Software and programming

Number representation

In the previous chapters we have described how, and why, a computer works in binary. Before we can describe the programming of a microprocessor, we must decide how we can represent binary numbers so we can recognise them.

Most microprocessors work with eight-bit data words and 16-bit addresses, so to the computer a store location is something like:

Address	Contents
1011 0111 0011 0110	1101 0110

which means little, even to the most experienced programmer! What we need is some shorthand way of representing binary numbers that is easy to recognise.

It might be thought that the easiest way would be simply to convert addresses and data to their decimal equivalents. The above would then be:

Address	Contents
46902	214

This would work, up to a point, but the relationship to the binary pattern is not obvious. The ideal representation needs to have an easy conversion method to binary, and decimal to binary conversion is somewhat tedious.

The method used universally by all microprocessor manufacturers is to split the binary number into blocks of four:

Address	Contents
1011 0111 0011 0110	1101 0110

This splitting is purely representational, and no physical division takes place inside the machine. Incidentally, with eight bits being called a byte, four bits is inevitably called a 'nibble'.

Four bits can represent from 0 to 15 in decimal. To save confusion using double digits, the numbers 10 to 15 are represented by the letters A to F. This is known as counting to base sixteen, or hex (for hexadecimal):

Binary	Decimal	Hex
0000	0	0
0001	1	1
0010	2	2
0011	3	3
0100	4	4
0101	5	5
0110	6	6
0111	7	7
1000	8	8
1001	9	9
1010	10	A
1011	11	B
1100	12	C
1101	13	D
1110	14	E
1111	15	F

It is now easy to go back to our binary numbers and represent them in hex:

Address	Contents
1011 0111 0011 0110	1101 0110
B 7 3 6	D 6

So address B736 contains D6. Note that it is very easy to go back from hex to binary. Simply write down the hex numbers and put the binary equivalent under each digit:

Address	Contents
0 C 5 0	A 9
0000 1100 0101 0000	1010 1001

Hex representation is used for all microprocessor instructions. In the Z-80, for example, the instruction to add one to the contents of register A is given as:

Increment A   3C

This means that if the microprocessor fetches an instruction from the store which has the bit pattern:

Hex   3   C
Binary   0011   1100

the control will add one to the contents of register A. The hex numbers given in microprocessor data books are simply a convenient way of representing binary numbers.

A programmer's view of a microcomputer

In Chapter 2 the hardware of a typical microcomputer was described. The programmer is not interested in details; to him or her the machine consists of the registers inside the CPU, the store location and the I/O. Most important of all, the programmer needs to know the form in which to write the instructions. The programmer would therefore view the

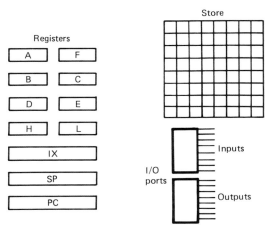

Figure 3.1. The programmer's view of a microcomputer

microcomputer of Chapter 2 in the somewhat simplistic form of *Fig. 3.1*.

It will be observed that *Fig. 3.1* has acquired two new registers, IX and SP. The use of these will be described later in this chapter.

Address modes

When the instructions available in microprocessors are examined the problem of the eight-bit word is encountered. Most microprocessors can address 64K, and as this requires 16 bits the instructions cannot be as simple as those adopted for Marvin in Chapter 1.

The different methods used to overcome these difficulties are known as 'address modes'. Those described below are available on most of the common microprocessors. All use one word to define the function (fetch, store, add, sub, etc.) plus several more words to define the address in one form or another. Unlike Marvin, a microprocessor instruction is *not* a constant length, and can occupy one, two, three or even four locations. This may appear a little confusing but in reality the different address modes are quite logical.

Implied
Examination of *Fig. 3.1* should indicate that many instructions will not need to access the store. Instructions in this category are data movements between registers, arithmetic functions between registers and control functions such as STOP.

These instructions are known as 'implied', because the data source and destination are inherently implied in the instruction (sometimes the term Register Direct is used). Since no address is needed, these instructions occupy a single store location. In the Z-80, for example:

    9B Add register A and B, result to register A
    4F Contents of register A to register C
    2C Add one to the contents of register L

These instructions all occupy one store location, and are efficient in the use of the store.

Immediate

Another set of instructions which do not access the store are those involving a constant. Typical examples are:

    Load A with constant 32
    Add 16 to register C

These instructions occupy two store locations, the first being the function code, the second the constant. Using the Z-80 again:

    3E n Load register A with n
    D6 n Subtract n from register A

The instruction is held in two successive store locations, so if we have:

    Address   Instruction
    0C50   3E 06

the store, in reality, contains:

    0C4F   –
    0C50   3E
    0C51   06
    0C52   –

After obeying 3E 06 the computer will obey the instruction in store location 0C52. The instruction, incidentally, will load the number six into register A.

Extended

Extended addressing is simply the addressing mode used by Marvin. The store address is given in its entirety. Since the function code takes one word, and two eight-bit words are needed for the address, extended addressing takes three store locations for each instruction. Some manufacturers use the term 'direct addressing'.

   From the Z-80 instruction set:

    C3 n n Jump to instruction at location n n
    32 n n Store the contents of register A in location n n
    3A n n Load register A with the contents of location n n

As before, because the instruction occupies three locations:

    Address   Instruction
    0D20   C3 10 F6

in the store is:

0D1F	–
0D20	C3
0D21	10
0D22	F6
0D23	–

which is a jump instruction to store location F610. Somewhat confusingly (but in fact logically), the least significant two hex digits are given first.

Relative addressing

Quite often programs do not need to specify actual store addresses, but can use expressions such as:

'If register A is positive, jump back 8 instructions'
or, 'Add the number 83 locations further on to register A'.
These instructions are using relative addressing because they are specifying store locations relative to the current location.

The number used is known as the 'offset', and most microprocessors use two words for a relative mode instruction: one word defines the function and one the offset. One word can hold a number from 0 to 255 or -128 to $+127$ if the offset is regarded as a signed binary number. The latter is used universally as it is more convenient to have both positive and negative offsets.

In the Z-80 instruction set, for example:

20 n Jump relative, offset n if register A is non-zero

The Z-80 defines the offset from the instruction following the relative jump, just to make things a little more complicated!

We can now write a simple program in Z-80 machine code.

Address	Instruction	Comment
0D00	3A 16 23	Load register A with contents of location 2316
0D03	D6 05	Subtract 5 from register A
0D05	2C	Add 1 to register L
0D06	20 FB	Jump non-zero relative, offset FB
0D08	3E 00	Clear register A (load with zero)
0D0A	C3 50 0C	Jump to instruction at location 0C50

54

Fig. 3.2 shows how this is held in the store.

Relative addressing allows programs to be written that can be located anywhere in the store, and which will then run without modification. Unfortunately relative addressing is one of the areas where microcomputers are decidedly inferior to their larger cousins. In larger computers relative

Location	Contents
0D00	3A
0D01	16
0D02	23
0D03	D6
0D04	05
0D05	2C
0D06	20
0D07	FB
0D08	3E
0D09	00
0D0A	C3
0D0B	50
0D0C	0C

Figure 3.2. Simple program held in store

addressing is allowed on all instructions which access the store. In most microcomputers relative addressing is only allowed on jumps.

Register indirect

It may have been noticed that the registers in *Fig. 3.1* are drawn in pairs; AF, BC, DE, HL. Most microprocessors allow these register pairs to be used to hold 16-bit data. These register pairs can be used to add, and manipulate, data in a similar manner to the eight-bit registers. Because 16 bits are needed to address 64K, they can also be used to hold addresses.

In register indirect addressing, instruction descriptions seem somewhat tortuous:

Add to register A the number whose address is held in register pair HL

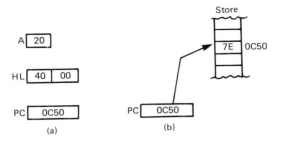

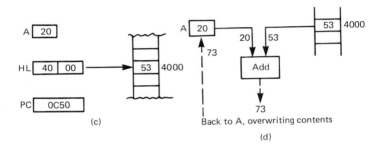

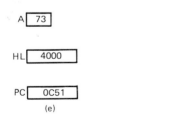

Figure 3.3. Register indirect addressing. (a) Initial conditions. (b) PC brings instruction (7E) and control decodes it. 7E is 'Add to A register HL indirect'. (c) Instruction is obeyed; HL addresses store, and brings contents of location 4000 to ALU. (d) Contents of location 4000 and A added. Result back to A. (e) PC is incremented ready for next instruction

> Jump to the instruction whose address is held in register pair BC

Register indirect addressing can be confusing on first encounter, so we will describe the step-by-step execution of a typical instruction. In the Z-80:

> 7E Add to register A, register HL indirect

Assume that register A contains a number, say 20 (hex), and we come to instruction 0C50:

Address	Instruction
0C50	7E

Control now looks at the register pair HL, and finds it contains 4000 (hex again). Control fetches the contents of location 4000, say 53, and adds them to the contents of register A to give 73 as the new contents of register A. This somewhat involved procedure is summarised on *Fig. 3.3*.

Mini- and mainframe computers allow indirect addressing with actual store locations holding the address of further store locations. These techniques are not for amateur programmers, and it is perhaps fortunate that the limitation of indirect addressing to register indirect was chosen by microprocessor designers

Register indirect addressing is very efficient in the use of the store, and particularly useful where a table of data is to be processed. The address of the first element of the table can be loaded into a register pair. Simple adds and subtracts on the register pair will then allow access to data in the table using register indirect instructions.

Indexed addressing

Indexed addressing is superficially very similar to register indirect addressing. It uses the new register IX in *Fig. 3.1* to hold what is known as the 'base address'. The base address holds a full 16-bit address.

An index addressed instruction requires two parts; one to define the function and one to hold an offset. The offset is added to (or subtracted from) register IX to give the store locations being accessed. This is best demonstrated by an example. In the Z-80 the function is defined by two words and the offset by one word. A typical instruction from the Z-80 set is:

    DD 7E d Load A indexed addressed offset d

An indexed addressed instruction thus occupies three store locations.

Suppose register IX contains 4D00 and the following instruction is obeyed:

    DD 7E 0A

The offset is 0A (decimal 10). This is added to the base address 4D00 to give 4D0A. The contents of store location 4D0A are brought to register A. The offset is a signed number in the range -128 to $+127$ similar to the offset for relative addressing.

Page zero mode

Page zero is the last addressing mode. A page zero addressed instruction can only access instructions in the memory range 0 to FF (decimal 255). Implementation of page zero mode varies from microprocessor to microprocessor. The 6502 uses a 'function-code, offset' type of instruction, with the offset defining the address in the range 0 to FF. The Z-80 only has eight page zero instructions. These are all single-word instructions, and call addresses:

    CF Call address 0008
    FF Call address 0038

General observations

Seven addressing modes have been described:

    i. Implied (register direct).
   ii. Immediate.
  iii. Extended (direct).
  iv. Relative.
   v. Register indirect.
  vi. Indexed.
 vii. Page zero.

These cover all the common address modes on microcomputers. It should be noted, however, that there are very real differences between their availability on different micro-processors. The 8080, for example, does not have relative addressing. An understanding of these basic addressing techniques should, however, allow the reader to follow the programming manuals for any machine.

The existence of variable length instructions obviously complicates the task of the microprocessor control logic. Having read the function word, it must not only decode the function, but also decide how many more words need to be brought down from the store to complete the instruction. Fortunately these complexities are solved by the micro-processor designer and need not concern the user.

The variable length instruction does mean, though, that a simple list of memory contents is really difficult to interpret.

```
0C50        3A
0C51        00
0C52        0D
0C53        06
0C54        FF
0C55        D1
0C56        E1
```

means little. Organising the list by instruction, thus:

```
0C50        3A  00  0D
0C53        06  FF
0C55        D1
0C56        E1
```

is a bit better, but still by no means easy to follow. Later in this chapter Assembly Languages, which improve the com-prehensibility of store listings, are described.

Microprocessor instruction sets

Marvin, our computer from Chapter 1, had ten types of instruction. A typical microprocessor has over a hundred. The Z-80, for example, has 158 official instructions (plus many unofficial ones). Many of these are simply variations on the same instruction (e.g. the same arithmetic function can be used in register direct, extended, indexed or immediate modes). In general, all instructions fall into seven simple categories:

   i. Data movement between stores and registers; sometimes called loads or moves.
   ii. Arithmetical operations.
   iii. Rotates and shifts.
   iv. Bit manipulation.
   v. Jumps and subroutines.
   vi. Input/output.
   vii. Control functions (such as STOP).

Loads and moves

In microprocessors, data movements are allowed between registers, and between registers and store locations. The addressing modes commonly available are: implied (for

Table 3.1. Z-80 8-bit loads

		IMPLIED		REGISTER							REG INDIRECT			INDEXED		EXT ADDR	IMME
		I	R	A	B	C	D	E	H	L	(HL)	(BC)	(DE)	(IX+d)	(IY+d)	(nn)	n
REGISTER	A	ED 57	ED 5F	7F	78	79	7A	7B	7C	7D	7E	0A	1A	DD 7E d	FD 7E d	3A n n	3E n
	B			47	40	41	42	43	44	45	46			DD 46 d	FD 46 d		06 n
	C			4F	48	49	4A	4B	4C	4D	4E			DD 4E d	FD 4E d		CE n
	D			57	50	51	52	53	54	55	56			FD 56 d	FD 56 d		16 n
	E			5F	58	59	5A	5B	5C	5D	5E			DD 5E d	FD 5E d		1E n
	H			67	60	61	62	63	64	65	56			DD 66 d	FD 66 d		26 n
	L			6F	68	69	6A	6B	6C	6D	6E			DD 6E d	FD 6E d		2E n
REG INDIRECT	(HL)			77	70	71	72	73	74	75							36 n
	(BC)			02													
	(DE)			12													
INDEXED	(IX+d)			DD 77 d	DD 70 d	DD 71 d	DD 72 d	DD 73 d	DD 74 d	DD 75 d							DD 36 d n
	(IY+d)			FD 77 d	FD 70 d	FD 71 d	FD 72 d	FD 73 d	FD 74 d	FD 75 d							FD 36 d n
EXT. ADDR	(nn)			32 n n													
IMPLIED	I			ED 47													
	R			ED 4F													

register to register), register indirect, indexed, extended addressed and immediate. Table 3.1 shows the eight-bit load group available on the Z-80. A few examples should explain the operation:

1E 57 loads register E with 57

4A moves the contents of register D to register C

32 6A 0D moves the contents of register A to store location 0D 6A

It was explained earlier that registers can be treated as 16-bit register pairs. Most microprocessors have a few restricted 16-bit load instructions. In the Z-80, for example, register pairs can be loaded with immediate data, or data can be moved between register pairs and two successive store locations. These instructions are four bytes long:

ED 48 3E 2C

will load data from 2C 3E to register L and from 2C 3F to register H.

There is also a special pair of 16-bit load instructions, known as 'push and pop' (some microprocessors call them 'push and pull'). These involve the stack pointer register SP that we introduced in *Fig. 3.1*, and will be described further when subroutines are discussed.

Arithmetical and logical operations

Although microprocessors have several registers, most arithmetical operations can only be performed on one register, usually denoted Register A or Acc. Addressing modes commonly employed are register direct, register indirect, indexed, immediate and extended. Table 3.2 shows the eight-bit arithmetic instructions for the Z-80. Note that the Z-80 does not permit extended addressing on arithmetical operations (although other microprocessors do).

The arithmetical functions Add and Subtract are provided on all microprocessors usually in two forms, Add (or Subtract) and Add (or Subtract) with carry. The simple operations add, or subtract, the specified data. When the arithmetic and carry operations are used, the carry flag from register F (see above) is added into the least significant bit with the data. This allows arithmetic to be performed with 16-bit numbers.

In addition to addition and subtraction, most micro-processors provide a few logical functions such as AND, OR, and Exclusive OR. These perform the logical operation on each bit of register A and the data, as summarised below:

Data	1011 0101
Register A	1100 0100
Result: AND	1000 0100
Result: OR	1111 0101
Result: XOR	0111 0001

Table 3.2. Z-80 8-bit arithmetic and logic

SOURCE

	REGISTER ADDRESSING							REG. INDIR.	INDEXED		IMMED
	A	B	C	D	E	H	L	(HL)	(IX+d)	(IY+d)	n
'ADD'	87	80	81	82	83	84	85	86	DD 86 d	FD 86 d	C6 n
ADD w CARRY 'ADC'	8F	88	89	3A	8B	8C	8D	8E	DD 8E d	FD 8E d	CE n
SUBTRACT 'SUB'	97	90	91	92	93	94	95	96	DD 96 d	FD 96 d	D6 n
SUB w CARRY 'SBC'	9F	98	99	9A	9B	9C	9D	9E	DD 9E d	FD 9E d	DE n
'AND'	A7	A0	A1	A2	A3	A4	A5	A6	DD A6 d	FD A6 d	E6 n
'XOR'	AF	A8	A9	AA	AB	AC	AD	AE	DD AE d	FD AE d	EE n
'OR'	B7	B0	B1	B2	B3	B4	B5	B6	DD B6 d	FD B6 d	F6 n
COMPARE 'CP'	BF	B8	B9	BA	BB	BC	BD	BE	DD BE d	FD BE d	FE n
INCREMENT 'INC'	3C	04	0C	14	1C	24	2C	34	DD 34 d	FD 34 d	
DECREMENT 'DEC'	3D	05	0D	15	1D	25	2D	35	DD 35 d	FD 35 d	

Many microprocessors have a Compare (or Test) instruction. This compares the contents of register A with the specified data and sets the flags in register F accordingly. The contents of register A are unaffected.

Finally, most microprocessors allow the contents of any register to be increased, or decreased, by one with a single byte instruction. These are known as incrementing and decrementing. From Table 3.2 we see, for example, that the instruction 2C will add one to the contents of register L.

In Chapter 2 we discussed the F (for flag) register, also known as the Condition Code Register in some micro-processors. All arithmetic operations set (or reset) the flags for use later in conditional jumps.

Rotates and shifts
This set of instructions could not be provided in Marvin because they can only be performed on binary numbers. They are based on two simple operations; shift up, and shift down. They simply shift the bit pattern in a register up, or down, by a specified number of places. Although basically a simple operation, there are many variations on what happens at the extreme ends of the register being shifted.

Logical shifts simply lose bits off one end and inject zero at the other. Arithmetic shifts maintain the sign (bit 7). Rotates

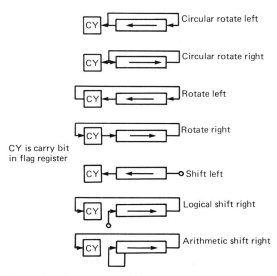

CY is carry bit in flag register

Figure 3.4. Rotates and shifts

63

(also known as cyclical shifts) link bit 7 and bit 0. These are summarised in *Fig. 3.4*.

At first sight rotates and shifts appear to be fairly useless luxuries, but consider the bit pattern:

01011010

This represents decimal 90. If we shift up one place we get:

10110100

which is decimal 180. Shifting up is equivalent to multiplying by two, shift right to dividing by two. Shifts can also be used with logical and arithmetic instructions to perform full multiplication and division.

When two decimal numbers are multiplied, we write something like:

```
          529
  ×        24
        ------
        10580
         2116
        ------
        12696
        ------
```

Binary numbers are multiplied in a similar manner:

```
         1011
  ×       101
        ------
       101100
        00000
         1011
        ------
       110111
        ------
```

It will be seen that this is a combination of shift, AND, and ADD instructions. A simplified flow chart for performing binary multiplication is given in *Fig. 3.5*.

Shifts can be performed in implied mode (with a one byte instruction causing a move of one place) or immediate mode

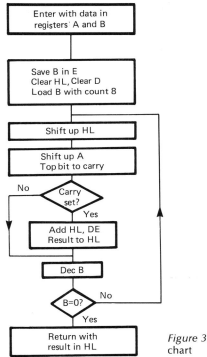

```
┌─────────────────────┐
│ Enter with data in  │
│ registers A and B   │
└─────────────────────┘

┌─────────────────────┐
│ Save B in E         │
│ Clear HL, Clear D   │
│ Load B with count 8 │
└─────────────────────┘

┌─────────────────────┐
│     Shift up HL     │
└─────────────────────┘
┌─────────────────────┐
│     Shift up A      │
│   Top bit to carry  │
└─────────────────────┘
        Carry
   No    set?
          Yes
┌─────────────────────┐
│     Add HL, DE      │
│    Result to HL     │
└─────────────────────┘

┌─────────────────────┐
│       Dec B         │
└─────────────────────┘
               No
         B=0?
          Yes
┌─────────────────────┐
│    Return with      │
│   result in HL      │
└─────────────────────┘
```

Figure 3.5. Multiplication flow chart

(with an offset giving the number of places). In theory, the number of places could be given indirectly by another register but this is rarely used in microprocessors.

Bit manipulation

In computing, bits in a word are often used to represent YES or NO. *Fig. 3.6* shows one possible way of representing data that might be used by a marketing firm. The data on each person could be held as one computer word.

This type of data is used in collation applications. A computer program could be written, for example, to sort out

65

from a mass of data the total number of bald-headed men with gloves between the ages of 25 and 35 living in Glasgow. To do this the computer needs to be able to set, reset, and test individual bits in the registers.

Bit manipulation is done by a simple, but comprehensive, range of instructions. Registers are defined by implied

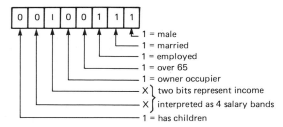

Person illustrated is a married male under 65, currently employed with salary in band 1, not an owner occupier, and with no children. This data is represented by the hex number 27.

Figure 3.6. Non-numerical data held in binary

addressing, and store location by register indirect and indexed addressing. By way of example, in the Z-80:

    CB 8B resets bit 1 in register E
    CB 5F sets the Z flag if bit 3 in register A is zero

The availability of bit manipulation instructions varies considerably between different machines. The 6502, for example, only has a bit instruction to mask the accumulator with some specified data. The Z-80 has the most powerful set of bit-related instructions, which makes it popular in industrial control where bits are used to represent plant limit switches and similar items. The 8080 has no bit manipulation instructions.

Jumps and subroutines
Conditional and unconditional jumps were described in Chapter 1 along with Marvin's other instructions. Microprocessors have similar jump instructions, but greater flexibility from their address modes and additional conditional

66

jumps. It should be noted that some manufacturers distinguish between conditional and unconditional jumps by the terms 'jump' and 'branch'.

Different microprocessors allow different address modes on jumps. Even within the same microprocessor different address modes are allowed on conditional and unconditional jumps. In the 6800, for example, all branch instructions use relative addressing, and the jump instruction uses indexed or extended addressing. In theory, extended, relative, register indirect, indexed and page zero can be used, but no microprocessor provides all modes on all jump instructions. This is one area where microcomputers are decidedly inferior to larger machines.

When we look at the conditions on branch instructions, we again have differences between microprocessors. Common conditions are: carry, no carry, zero, non-zero, sign negative, sign positive. Some machines provide combination tests such as less than, or equal to, zero. Again, microprocessors are inferior to larger machines in the provision of conditional jumps.

Fig. 3.5 showed a flow chart for multiplying two binary numbers. It would be wasteful to have to write commonly-used routines each time they are used in a program. All microprocessors (and all computers) provide instructions to allow commonly-used routines (such as multiplication, division and binary to decimal conversion) to be written once, and then called an unlimited number of times in the program. This operation is known as calling subroutines.

The operation of subroutines is very simple, and is summarised in *Fig. 3.7*. Between location 4000 and 4100 we have written a subroutine to multiply the numbers in register A and register B, and giving the result in HL. The main program proceeds until it comes to 0C50 where a multiplication is required. The instruction in 0C50 calls the subroutine (in a manner yet to be described) and the program jumps to 4000. At the end of the subroutine, the program jumps back to the instruction after 0C50.

The program proceeds until it reaches 0D00 where another multiplication is required. The program again goes to 4000, but this time, at the end of the subroutine, the program returns to the instruction after 0D00. Obviously, the subroutine must establish in some manner the point in the main program to return to when the subroutine is complete.

The return from a subroutine is done in a simple but ingenious manner by using part of the store as a 'stack' and the SP register (for stack pointer) shown in *Fig. 3.1.*

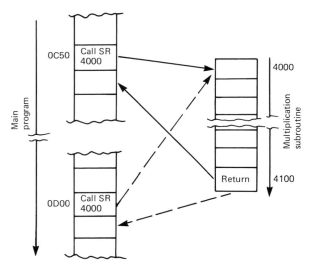

Figure 3.7. Subroutines

The stack is an area of store used to hold return addresses from subroutines. Normally the stack starts at the top of the store and works down. The stack pointer register holds the current address of the end of the stack.

The sequence of operations in performing a call to, and return from, a subroutine at address 4EC3 is summarised below. At the start of the sequence the first free space in the stack is at FFF8 (near the top of a 64K store), and the call subroutine instruction is at 0C50:

i. Program counter contents (0C50) are placed in FFF8 and FFF7. FFF8 now contains 0C and FFF7 contains 50.

ii. Stack pointer is decremented twice to give FFF6 (the next free location in the stack). (Actually steps i and ii are simultaneous rather than sequential.)

iii. The subroutine address (4000) is placed in the program counter.

iv. Subroutine instruction obeyed.

v. At the end of the subroutine, a RETURN instruction instructs the microprocessor that the subroutine is complete. Stack pointer contains FFF6 at this point.

vi. The contents of FFF7 and FFF8 are brought to the program counter which now contains 0C50.

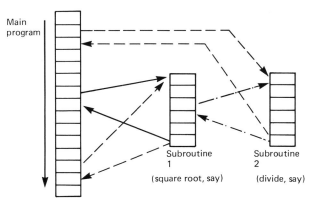

Figure 3.8. Nesting of subroutines

vii. The stack pointer is incremented twice to give FFF8 again.

viii. The program counter is increased by the length of the call subroutine instruction (say three locations) to give 0C53, the address of the next instruction.

ix. Main program continues.

The operation of putting an address on to the stack is often called a 'push'. The retrieval of an address from the stack is called a 'pull' or 'pop'. The use of the stack allows sub-routines to call subroutines as shown in *Fig. 3.8*. The only practical limit is the amount of store that can be allocated to the stack. This is known as nesting of subroutines.

Table 3.3. Z-80 jump and subroutine calls

			CONDITION									
			UN-COND	CARRY	NON CARRY	ZERO	NON ZERO	PARITY EVEN	PARITY ODD	SIGN NEG	SIGN POS	REG B=0
JUMP 'JP'	IMMED EXT.	nn	C3 n n	DA n n	D2 n n	CA n n	C2 n n	EA n n	E2 n n	FA n n	F2 n n	
JUMP 'JP'	RELATIVE	PC+e	18 e-2	38 e-2	30 e-2	28 e-2	20 e-2					
JUMP 'JP'		(HL)	E9									
JUMP 'JP'	REG. INDIR.	(IX)	DD E9									
JUMP 'UP'		(IY)	FD E9									
'CALL'	IMMED. EXT.	nn	CD n n	DC n n	D4 n n	CC n n	C4 n n	EC n n	E4 n n	FC n n	F4 n n	
DECREMENT B, JUMP IF NON ZERO 'DJNZ'	RELATIVE	PC+e										10 e-2
RETURN 'RET'	REGISTER INDIR.	(SP) (SP+1)	C9	D8	D0	C8	C0	EB	E0	F8	F0	
RETURN FROM INT 'RETI'	REG. INDIR.	(SP) (SP+1)	ED 4D									
RETURN FROM NON MASKABLE INT 'RETN'	REG. INDIR.	(SP) (SP+1)	ED 45									

All microprocessors have conditional calls to subroutines and conditional returns. Usually extended or indexed addressing is used for the call instruction and a single-byte implied instruction for the return. Table 3.3 shows the jumps and subroutine calls available on a Z-80.

Input and output
Input and output instructions are one area where there are significant differences between different microprocessors. It was explained in Chapter 1 that there is a vast difference in speed between the microprocessor and even the fastest peripheral device. In general this speed difference is resolved by the interface electronics, and is not the direct concern of the programmer (except that it will be necessary to check to see if the peripheral is ready to receive or give

data by obtaining a status signal from the device). The actual interfacing is described further in Chapters 4 and 5.

Every external device has an address (called a port) so the computer will issue instructions such as:

'Output the character in register A to the teletype on port 3'

'Read the state of the 8 switches on port 5 into register L'

The major differences between microprocessors is the way in which the addresses are derived.

Some microprocessors deal with input/output addresses as part of the computer memory, and data transfer takes place with the normal load (move) instructions described earlier. A microcomputer with this approach is the Motorola 6800. This technique does have some advantages; the computer's range of addressing modes is available, and instructions such as:

'Add the number from port 316 to register A'

can be performed directly. The major disadvantage is that an I/O device cannot share the same address as a store location. This is of no great concern to the home-computer user, but can be awkward in a large industrial control system needing a large store and a vast array of input/output ports.

The second approach (used by the Z-80) is to have separate store and input/output control signals. The Z-80 can support store locations and I/O ports with the same address. The range of input/output instructions is, however, somewhat restrictive, since only IN and OUT are provided with direct, or register indirect, addressing.

Control instructions

Most microprocessors have a small range of control instructions. These include the very important 'STOP' or the useful 'No operation' (known as NOP on most machines, and used to leave gaps in programs for correcting programming mistakes at a later date!).

Many control instructions are particular to one microprocessor. The Z-80, for example, has two identical sets of registers, although the microprocessor can only work with one set at a time. The programmer can switch register sets with an EX (for exchange) instruction.

A useful symbolism

Some of the instruction descriptions can be long-winded, so it is useful to have a symbolic way of writing computer operations. There are many different ways of representing operations, but a common standard starts with the backward arrow ← to represent the computer operation. The start conditions are to the right of the arrow, and the end conditions to the left. Registers are represented by their letters so:

A ← B

moves the contents of register B to register A (in many respects, the arrow can be thought of as 'becomes').

A ← 15

thus loads A with the number 15 (load A immediate 15), and

A ← A + C

adds the contents of register C to register A.

Store locations are indicated by parentheses, so:

A ← (0C50)

loads register A with the contents of store location 0C50, and:

(0D00) ← C

puts the contents of register C in store location 0D00.

A ← A + (HL)

adds the contents of the store location whose address is held in the register pair HL to the contents of register A.

Note the important difference between:

A ← 15

and A ← (15)

Indexed instructions can be represented as:

C ← (IX + 4)

where 4 is the offset to be added to the index register contents to give the address.

To avoid confusion with the addition sign, Λ is commonly used for AND and V used for OR. (The dot . is also used sometimes for AND.) The $\oplus$ symbol is used for exclusive OR. Typical logic equations could be:

A ← A Λ B
B ← B V (HL)

Microprocessor data books often express the instructions available in this symbolic form.

Assembly languages

Writing a program in hex coding is possibly instructive, but it is certainly time-consuming and error-prone. No programmer can ever learn all the codings for one microprocessor, so programming at this level becomes a continual flicking through dog-eared data sheets.

Because actual store location addresses are used, a very simple program change (inserting, say, one instruction omitted in error) will affect the addresses of every subsequent instruction, and necessitate many changes to other parts of the program.

There is also a very real possibility that a program will self-destruct when first run. Every number means something to the computer, so if a jump instruction is one location out, the computer could jump to the middle of an instruction. Suppose we have in a Z-80:

```
0C50      3A ⎤
0C51      4A ⎬   3A 4A 86
0C52      86 ⎦
```

which is 'load register A with the contents of location 864A'. A programmer intends to jump, with a relative jump, to 0C50, but miscalculates the offset and jumps to 0C51. The computer will take 4A as an instruction rather than part of an address (this is C ← D actually in Z-80 coding). Clearly the program is off the rails, and will probably overwrite itself in a very short time. Errors such as this can be very difficult to find as the machine destroys the evidence!

Programming in hex coding is known as machine-code programming, and is rarely done by professional programmers. Most programs are written in a form much easier to follow, and the computer itself used to write the machine-code program.

The use of mnemonics
Dictionaries define a mnemonic as an aid to memory. There are really very few basic instructions in a microprocessor, but many variations. By taking the symbolism idea outlined earlier, and combining it with an easily remembered mnemonic such as ADD,LD, IN, etc, we can represent instructions in an easily recognisable form:

LD A, B	Contents of register B moved to register A
LD (HL), A	Contents of register A stored in the store location whose address is held in the register pair HL (indirect addressing)
ADD A, 155	Add 155 to the contents of register A (load immediate)

Surprisingly few mnemonics are needed to cover the vast range of instructions. The Z-80, for example, uses about 25 mnemonics, with address modes being described by careful use of register letters and brackets.

The use of mnemonics is the first stage in building an assembly language. The next stage is the use of 'labels' to identify store locations. Labels are names the programmer uses to refer to a store location. These names can be anything the programmer wishes so store locations could be called START or BILL or THING 1 or SPEED. It should be emphasised that these names are purely paper references and no such names are, in reality, attached to the location in the machine.

The programmer can now write:

ADD A, BILL

which means 'add to register A the contents of the store location whose label is BILL'. Sensible use of labels adds considerably to the understanding of a program.

The use of mnemonics and labels obviously makes a program easier to follow, but before it can run, the program has to be converted into the corresponding machine codes. This is done by a special program called an 'assembler'. This is a machine code program supplied (at a suitable price) by a computer manufacturer. The assembler is loaded into the computer, and started. The programmer types in his program complete with mnemonics and labels. The assembler stores the program in mnemonic form. When all the program is in, the programmer instructs the computer to start the conversion. The assembler now goes through the mnemonics and labels, and produces the corresponding machine-code program.

To show how this works, here is how a Z-80 assembler produces a machine-code subroutine to multiply two eight-bit numbers. This will follow the flow chart of *Fig. 3.5* but there are a few practical points to note.

A single instruction typed into the Assembler has the form:

    Line number   Label   Mnemonic   Comments

The label and comments are optional, the line number and instruction mnemonic mandatory. A label, if present, can have up to four letters or numbers, but the first character must be a letter. Comments are preceded by a semi-colon, the assembler ignoring the rest of the line. Comments, though optional, should be freely used.

The line numbers tell the assembler the order in which the instructions are to be taken. It is not necessary (or even desirable) for these to go up in steps of one, since they are taken in ascending order. It is usual to use steps of ten initially to leave gaps for easy error correction. If the instruction below were entered:

Line number	Instruction
40	LD A, 5
70	LD B, A
55	ADD A, C

The assembler would put the instructions in the order:

40	LD A, 5
55	ADD A, C
70	LD B, A

We must tell the assembler where the program is to be put in the store. This is done by a pseudo-instruction ORG (for Origin) followed by the location for the first instruction. ORG H 1234˙ would cause the assembler to put the first instruction at location 1234 hex (H means the number is in hex).

Fig. 3.9 shows the mnemonic instructions typed into the assembler. This is known as the source program. The actual subroutine occupies lines 100 to 210. A small test program was added at lines 300 to 340 so the subroutine could be tested.

```
LINE          SOURCE
100           ORG H4000
110    MULT   LD D,0        ;THESE LINES
120           LD E,B        ;INITIALISE
130           LD HL,0       ;REGISTERS
140           LD B,8        ;COUNTER IN REG B
150    LOOP   ADD HL,HL     ;SHIFT UP HL
160           RLA           ;TOP BIT TO CARRY
170           JP NC,SKIP    ;TEST TOP BIT
180           ADD HL,DE     ;TOP BIT WAS 1
190    SKIP   DEC B         ;DEC COUNTER
200           JP NZ,LOOP    ;ALL DONE?
210           RET           ;YES
220  ;TEST PROG FOLLOWS
230  ;CHANGE DATA AT LINES 310,320
300           ORG H3000
310           LDA,5         ;TEST DATA IN A
320           LDB,3         ;TEST DATA IN B
330           CALL MULT     ;CALL SUBROUTINE
340           HALT          ;END
```

Figure 3.9. Assembler source program

Line 100 sets the first location of the subroutine at hex 4000, and line 300 sets the first location of the small test program to hex 3000. The Z-80 does not have shifts for register pairs, so a shift up of HL is achieved at line 150 by adding HL to HL: a typical example of the restrictions of microcomputer programming.

The mnemonics should be fairly obvious. Lines 110, 130, 140, 310 and 320 are immediate mode. Lines 170 and 200 are conditional jumps, with labels for the destination addresses.

LOC	OBJ	LINE		SOURCE	
4000		100		ORG H4000	
4000	1600	110	MULT	LD D,0	;THESE LINES
4002	58	120		LD E,B	;INITIALISE
4003	210000	130		LD HL,0	;REGISTERS
4006	0608	140		LD B,8	;COUNTER IN REG B
4008	29	150	LOOP	ADD HL,HL	;SHIFT UP HL
4009	17	160		RLA	;TOP BIT TO CARRY
400A	D20E40	170		JP NC,SKIP	;TEST TOP BIT
400D	19	180		ADD HL,DE	;TOP BIT WAS 1
400E	05	190	SKIP	DEC B	;DEC COUNTER
400F	C20840	200		JP NZ,LOOP	;ALL DONE?
4012	C9	210		RET	;YES
4012		220		;TEST PROG FOLLOWS	
4012		230		;CHANGE DATA AT LINES 310,320	
3000		300		ORG H3000	
3000	3E05	310		LDA,5	;TEST DATA IN A
3002	0603	320		LDB,3	;TEST DATA IN B
3004	CD0040	330		CALL MULT	;CALL SUBROUTINE
3007	C7	340		HALT	;END

ASSEMBLY COMPLETE, NO ERRORS

Figure 3.10. Assembler object program

NC stands for 'No Carry' and NZ for 'No Zero'. RLA is a rotate left (shift) on register A, with the top bit going into the carry flag in register F.

CALL MULT means 'go to the subroutine starting at the label MULT'. RET means return from subroutine. All comments after the semicolons are ignored by the assembler.

With the source program typed in, the assembler is instructed to commence the conversion. The assembler produces (assembles) the machine-code program (known as the Object Program) on tape, disc or direct to RAM, and produces a listing as shown in *Fig. 3.10*.

The machine-code program is given under OBJ (for Object Program). The store locations are given under LOC. The original source program is given as well. During assembly, checks are made for errors in the source program. Common faults are unspecified labels (e.g. LD A, FRED, with FRED not given elsewhere) and misspelt mnemonics. Most assemblers are very strict on their 'grammar'. The assembly operation in *Fig. 3.9* was successful and no errors found. Incidentally, this is no guarantee that the program will run as intended; it merely means that it contains no grammatical errors.

At any time the source program (in mnemonics) can be saved on tape or disc. If the object program goes off the rails, or does not work correctly, the source program can be reloaded in a few minutes and corrections made. All assemblers have editing facilities to allow lines to be corrected and new instructions added. Remember the cautious programmer originally wrote the source program with line numbers going up in tens, so there is plenty of scope for additional instructions.

We have only scratched the surface of assemblers. Even the simplest assembler has facilities that would take a chapter of this book to describe. Important topics we have not covered are the ways relative jumps are coded in assembler languages, and the way an intelligent assembler can handle locations relative to a label (e.g. LD A, FRED + 3). It should be obvious, however, that an assembler is essential for anyone attempting extensive machine-code programming.

Monitors

A very reasonable question to ask at this point would be how a program gets into the RAM in the first place, and how the microprocessor is told where to start the program.

In a dedicated system, where the computer only does one job, the program will be held in a ROM, so there is no problem loading the program. All microprocessors have a control signal pin called Reset, or some similar title. When this pin is energised, the program counter is set to zero causing the program to start at the instruction at location zero. If the program ROM is placed at the bottom addresses of the store, a jump instruction to the actual program can be placed at address zero in the ROM. Usually the reset line is strobed at power turn-on by a simple resistor-capacitor circuit, forcing the computer to start at the correct point each time it is switched on.

A general-purpose computer, however, will operate with many different programs. These machines are initially controlled by a program supplied by the computer manufacturer. This program, often called a monitor (or bug), is held in ROM starting at address zero. The monitor program is therefore entered automatically when the microprocessor reset line is strobed on power-up.

To describe how this monitor program works, consider a hypothetical general-purpose microcomputer consisting of a box (containing the microprocessor, power supply, store and I/O logic), a visual display unit (or VDU), a tape recorder for bulk storage of programs and a keyboard, via which the operator/programmer can communicate with the machine.

When turned on, the computer enters the monitor program as described above. A very simple monitor program gives the programmer the following options:

    i. Modify a store location.
    ii. Execute a program.
    iii. Write a program to the cassette.
    iv. Read a program from the cassette.

The programmer chooses his option by typing the initial letter (M, E, W or R) followed by relevant data. The modify option is used to load a machine-code program, so let us follow what happens if a small machine-code program is loaded. On power-up the monitor program puts up a greeting and a colon : as a prompt to show it is ready for commands. In the dialogue below, computer messages are underlined, user replies not underlined. This does *not* occur on the VDU, it is merely to show who is saying what. Each line is ended by the operator pressing the ENTER key. We turn the machine on:

HELLO

: M3000

3000 F7 : 3E 05

The operator wanted to modify location hex 3000, the computer replied that location 3000 currently held F7. The operator altered location 3000 to 3E, and 3001 to 05, by entering the machine-code instruction 3E 05. We now enter the remaining instructions:

: M3002

3002 B2 : 06 03

: M3004

3004 15 : CD 00 40

: M3007

3007 2A : C7

All the program is now in, and the operator wishes to run it. He types E (for execute) followed by the start location:

: E 3000

The monitor program now jumps to location 3000, and starts to obey the user's program. Note that the user's program is running now, not the monitor program.

Most microcomputers have a reset push-button in some form to allow the user to regain control of a program that is off the rails. This strobes the reset pin on the microprocessor causing the monitor program to be re-entered.

With the program working correctly, the operator now wishes to save it on tape. He uses the Write command, and instructs the computer where the program starts and finishes. The reset button is pressed to go back to the monitor, and:

HELLO

: W 3000 3007

START TAPE PRESS ENTER WHEN RUNNING

The computer now starts to write the program to the tape, and informs the operator when it has finished:

DONE, TURN TAPE OFF

:

The colon prompt means the editor is ready for further commands.

A program is loaded from tape in a similar manner, except that the tape itself gives the start and finish locations. The operator now loads his tape, to check if the recording was successful:

: R

START TAPE, PRESS ENTER WHEN RUNNING

The program is loaded

LOADED 3000 3007 NO ERRORS, TURN TAPE OFF

: E 3000

After the last prompt, the operator types E3000 to start his own program running again.

Most microcomputers have monitors with far more facilities than the simple example above. A very useful facility is the ability to stop a user's program at a predetermined point and display the contents of all the registers. This is called a

'Breakpoint'. Another useful facility is 'Single Step', by which a programmer can execute his program one instruction at a time, examining the register contents at each step.

The facilities offered by monitors vary considerably, from the simple M, E, W, R type described above to complex monitors with built-in assembler. There is, of course, a direct relationship between the facilities offered and the cost of the computer!

High-level languages

Programming a computer in assembly language is far simpler than machine-code programming, but is still very tedious and error-prone. The programmer has to write one source statement for each machine-code instruction, and keep careful track of the store locations and labels used.

If an assembler program can convert mnemonics and labels to machine-code instructions, it is reasonable to ask if it is possible to obtain a program to convert directly from mathematical expressions to machine code. Such programs are called high-level languages.

Suppose we want to add two numbers together (in store locations BILL and FRED) and want to put the result in a store location JOHN. In assembler language we would write:

```
110 LD A, BILL
120 ADD A, FRED
130 LD JOHN, A
```

and we would need to ensure that register A was not holding anything required later, before the first load was obeyed. We can postulate a high-level language where we could write:

```
100 JOHN = FRED + BILL
```

The computer would convert our high-level source statement into the corresponding machine-code program, and we would not have to worry about the actual register contents.

The above example was fairly trivial, but high-level languages contain subroutines for multiply and divide, and most will also have subroutines for various mathematical functions such as square roots, sines, cosines, etc. The programmer can thus write complex statements such as:

200 OUTPUT = (GAIN * INPUT)/(1 + GAIN * FBACK)

directly, and leave the high-level language to sort out the machine-code instruction and subroutines.

In use, a high-level language is very similar to an assembler. The high-level language program is loaded into the computer (often it is held permanently in a ROM). The programmer then loads his high-level source program, which is then converted into machine-code instructions in a similar manner to an assembler.

There are, however, two ways in which a high-level language source program can be converted to machine code. A high-level language compiler converts the entire program to a machine-code object program in the same way as an assembler. The object program can be written out to disc or tape for later use, and the source program discarded.

A high-level language interpreter holds the source program in RAM at all times, and produces machine-code instructions for each line of source program as it is needed. This approach greatly simplifies the design of the manufacturer's high-level language program, but has several major disadvantages. Because the source program is held at all times, it is very wasteful of store space. In addition, because the computer has to examine each line of source program, convert it to machine code and obey it at the time of execution, interpreters are very, very slow.

Compilers are at least as efficient as a good programmer, and produce compact, fast, machine-code programs. They are, however, quite complicated to write and are correspondingly expensive.

For most small domestic or business microcomputers the cost advantages of an interpreter far outweigh the disadvantages. The vast majority of high-level languages run on microcomputers therefore operate as interpreters. Professional programmers on larger machines, where speed is all important, use compilers.

BASIC, a typical high-level language

In a book of this size, it is not possible to give a detailed account of any high-level language. A quick description of BASIC, the language used on most home computers, should, however, give an appreciation of the ease with which high-level language programs can be written. (For more details, see the companion volume *Beginner's Guide to Basic Programming*.)

In BASIC all store locations are referred to by names chosen by the programmer, so BILL or SPEED or A or T2 are all legitimate names. Unlike an assembler, however, the computer allocates the store addresses and the programmer does not need to know where his data is held. All BASICs will handle numbers considerably in excess of the 0–255 that can be held in a single eight-bit location. A store name will, in fact, refer to at least three actual store locations.

BASIC instructions start with a line number. These are used by the computer to indicate the execution order in exactly the same manner as line numbers in assembly languages.

The simplest BASIC instruction is LET, which is used for mathematical expressions. BASIC works entirely in decimal, and does all its decimal/binary/decimal conversions without the user's knowledge. A simple BASIC instruction could be:

    10 LET A = 3

This will take a block of store locations, call them A and put the value 3 into the block. (A block of store locations is used to allow numbers considerably larger than 255 to be stored.) Another simple instruction:

    20 LET BILL = 7

This will put 7 into a block of store locations with the name BILL. The LET instrument can also use the four mathematical symbols:

+ Addition
− Subtraction
* Multiplication
/ Division

We can therefore write expressions such as:

84

30 LET JOE = A + BILL

This will take the numbers in A and BILL, add them and put the result in a new location JOE. The contents of locations A and BILL are unaffected.

Where there is any possibility of confusion, parentheses ( ) can be used. For example:

LET C = JOE + (A/2)
and LET C = (JOE + A) /2

Although BASIC does define the order of execution without parentheses, it makes the program easier to read later if they are used.

The right-hand side of a LET statement can be any reasonable length and complexity. The same name can appear on both sides of the equals sign:

40 LET SPEED = SPEED + 10

is quite legitimate.

The next instruction is PRINT. In its simplest form it will print the contents of a store location on a printer or VDU screen:

50 PRINT JOE

will print the contents of store location block JOE.

We can now put a simple program together:

10 LET A = 3
20 LET B = 7
30 LET C = B − A
40 LET D = (C × 9) /A
50 PRINT C
60 PRINT D

When run, this would produce the results:

4
12

The PRINT statement can also be used to write messages by enclosing the text within quotes " ". For example:

25 PRINT "HELLO FOLKS"

would print the message:

HELLO FOLKS

The next instruction allows us to input data from the keyboard. The INPUT statements takes a number from the keyboard, and puts it into the specified location. For example:

10 INPUT BILL

will take a number typed at the keyboard and put it in the store location with the name BILL.

All computer programs require some form of conditional jump. In BASIC this is privided by the IF statement, which usually takes the form:

IF (condition) GOTO (line number)

Conditions are combinations of $<>$ or $=$. For example:

80 IF SUM $<$ BILL GOTO 150

An unconditional jump is allowed, and takes the form GOTO (line number):

90 GOTO 450

We can now write a small program to print out multiplication tables.

```
10 PRINT "WHICH TIMES TABLE"
20 INPUT N
30 LET MULT = 1
40 LET RES = N × MULT
50 PRINT RES
60 LET MULT = MULT + 1
70 IF MULT < = 10 GOTO 40
80 STOP
```

The program incorporates a loop at lines 40 to 70 which is executed ten times. The purpose of line 80 is obvious.

BASIC has many additional facilities (which allow the above program to be written with far fewer lines). Further description of BASIC would turn this book into a BASIC textbook rather than an introduction to microprocesors. There are many excellent textbooks on BASIC, and the interested reader should refer to these.

The diversion into BASIC was included to demonstrate the ease with which high-level language programs can be written. The author has been involved with introducing computers to non-technical people, and experience suggests that people can usually write useful BASIC programs after an hour or so at a computer. It is also interesting to observe how ten- and eleven-year-old children take to high-level programming like ducks to water.

A question the author has often been asked by people who have tried BASIC programming for the first time is, 'Is that really all there is to it? It's too easy'. The answer is always 'Yes, once you brush away preconceived notions of difficulty, it really is that easy'.

A cautionary note

One of the supposed advantages of a high-level language is the portability of programs. Unlike assembly language programs which are specific to one machine, high-level language programs should run on any machine.

In practice this is not always true as there are many variations on even a simple language such as BASIC. Many so called Tiny BASICS will only handle integers (whole numbers) in the range $\pm$ 32 000, so data such as 16.327 would be truncated to 16, and data such as 68 236 would bring up an error message. In general, BASICs occupying under 3K of ROM use integer arithmetic.

There are also many dialect differences between different versions of the same language. Usually a program written for one machine can be made to run on another, but often a fair number of minor corrections need to be made.

Finally, quite a few programs are totally untransferable because of the way the program is written around characteristics of a specific machine. The PET computer, for example, has a wide range of graphic symbols (clubs, hearts, men, etc.). Another popular machine, the TRS-80, has only set/reset graphics (see Chapter 4 for details of VDUs). A program written to take advantage of the PET graphics could not be transferred directly to a TRS-80.

Other languages

BASIC is the most popular computer language for home and small business machines, but its limitations make it somewhat unpopular with professional programmers. Because it is an interpreter, BASIC is slow and wasteful of store space. Many other languages exist, both as compilers and interpreters, and it is a credit to BASIC's simplicity that it survives despite its shortcomings.

One language that is making a challenge is PASCAL. This is a descendant of the scientific language ALGOL and seems to meet the requirements of professional programmers in that it uses a very efficient structured form. It is, however, not as easy to learn as BASIC which has not made it as popular with the amateur user.

Other popular languages encountered on microcomputers are FORTH (which uses the concept of a stack to hold values, and allows the programmer to define his own words) and the educational language LOGO. The latter, in its simplest form, allows primary-school children to write graphics programs and is an excellent introduction to computing.

The classical high-level languages, ALGOL, FORTRAN and COBOL, are almost unknown at the middle and bottom end of the microcomputer market, which is not really surprising as it would be nearly impossible to run them without some form of backing store. The UK language CORAL, designed for industrial control, is very popular in that field, but is not really suitable for business or home use.

High-level languages do not have to use English or mathematical symbols. In Chapter 6 we will encounter an industrial control language, GEM-80, which uses process-control symbols to form computer programs.

Writing programs

Starting to write a program can be a daunting task similar to starting to write a book. A crude attempt to write a program from scratch in one go will be doomed to failure. Fortunately there are three methods commonly used to simplify the task. All require the programmer to plan his work.

Flow charts are the commonest technique, and are particularly popular as they allow the programmer to visualise his program. An example of flowcharting was shown in *Fig. 3.5.* Usually, increasingly more complicated flowcharts are produced until the point is reached where the flowchart can be easily converted into program instructions.

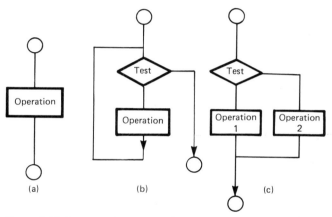

Figure 3.11. Structured program elements. *(a)* Simple operation. *(b)* Do While. *(c)* If Then Else

The second technique is called Modular Programming, and is suited to large programs written by several people. The program is split into identifiable blocks which are written separately (e.g. a binary to BCD block or a keyboard input block). These blocks are joined together to form the program. An advantage of this method is the library of routines that rapidly builds up for use in future programs.

The final, somewhat specialised, technique is called Structured Programming. Hailed by some as the ultimate programming tool (but thought by many to be ridiculously complex), it forces the programmer to think logically. Programs constructed with flow charts or modules tend to become untidy octopuses which can be difficult to debug. It can be shown that any program can be written using the three blocks of *Fig. 3.11*. Each of these blocks has one input and one output, so a program written around them will be a simple to follow progression.

Inexperienced programmers find structured programs awkward to write, and some languages, such as BASIC, are not really suitable for this technique. Structured programs are best suited to ALGOL and PASCAL languages which have been written specifically for a structured approach. It is fair to say that structured programming is preferred by professional programmers.

Whatever approach is used, it is essential to provide good documentation. All programs require modifications during initial testing, and this is considerably simplified by having an explanation of how it is *supposed* to work. Documentation is also invaluable if any future changes are to be made. Too often, however, the documentation provided by most programmers is minimal.

4

Peripherals

Any computer must be able to communicate with the outside world. This communication can, in general, take two forms. The first occurs where the computer is used to control equipment or industrial plant. The computer communicates with a wide range of devices including limit switches, transducers, electric motors, etc. This form of input and output is known as industrial control, and is covered in Chapter 5.

The second form of communication takes place between the computer and people. The computer thus utilises printers, VDUs, keyboards and other devices known collectively as peripherals. This chapter discusses the peripherals that are found on a typical microcomputer. We must however first discuss the basic ideas of how input and output are achieved on a microcomputer.

Ports and addresses

On most microcomputers, all input data and output data is handled in eight-bit words (called bytes). Each peripheral device thus receives or transmits data as a sequence of eight-bit words. In most systems the data will be text in one form or another, and eight bits can be coded to cover the full range of alphabetic symbols in upper and lower case, numerals 0 to 9, punctuation marks and control signals such as new line, delete, sound bell etc. The actual coding commonly used is called ASCII, (for American Standard Code for Information Interchange) and is reproduced in Table 4.1.

It was explained earlier that an I/O device has an address similar to a store location. This address is known as a port. A

Table 4.1. Hex to ASCII coding

00	NUL	21	!	42	B	63	c
01	SOH	22	-	43	C	64	d
02	STX	23	#	44	D	65	e
03	ETX	24	ß	45	E	66	f
04	EOT	25	%	46	F	67	g
05	ENQ	26	&	47	G	68	h
06	ACK	27	'	48	H	69	i
07	BEL	28	(	49	I	6A	j
08	BS	29	)	4A	J	68	k
09	HT	2A	*	4B	k	6C	l
0A	LF	2B	+	4C	L	6D	m
0B	VT	2C		4D	M	6E	n
0C	FF	2D	−	4E	N	6F	o
0D	CR	2E	.	4F	O	70	p
0E	SO	2F	/	50	P	71	q
0F	SI	30	0	51	Q	72	r
10	DLE	31	†	52	R	73	s
11	DC1	32	2	53	S	74	t
12	DC2	33	3	54	T	75	u
13	DC3	34	4	55	u	76	v
14	DC4	35	5	56	V	77	w
15	NAK	36	6	57	W	78	x
16	SYN	37	7	58	X	79	y
17	ETB	38	8	59	Y	7A	z
18	CAN	39	9	5A	Z	7B	(
19	EM	3A	:	5B	[	7C	
1A	SUB	3B	;	5C		7D	}
1B	ESC	3C	<	5D	]		
1C	FS	3D	=	5E	?(↑)	7E	
1D	GS	3E	>	5F	—(←)	7F	DEL
1E	RS	3F	?	60	`		(RUB OUT)
1F	US	40	(u	61	a		
20	SPACE	41	A	62	b		

peripheral thus connects to the computers three highways as shown in *Fig. 4.1*, with the transmitted (or received) data flowing on the data bus. Some microcomputers treat ports and store locations in the same way, and use load (or move) instructions to input or output data. This is known as 'memory mapped' I/O. The Motorola 6800 is one common microprocessor using this principle. With a large number of peripherals this can prove inconvenient as ports and store locations cannot share addresses.

Some microprocessors have separate input/output control lines, and microprocessors such as the Z-80 can, in theory, have 64K of store and 255 port addresses. These microprocessors have separate IN and OUT instructions.

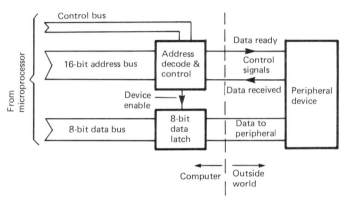

Figure 4.1. Interface logic

In *Fig. 4.1* there are control signals labelled 'device enable'. These are driven by the address decode logic, and are enabled when the port's address is selected. Usually the address decode logic will incorporate wire links or miniature switches on which the port address can be set up.

Quite often one peripheral device can be connected to two, or more, port addresses. A printer, for example, can receive data on one address, and transmit status data (e.g. busy, fault, out of paper) on another address. Usually these two addresses will be sequential (e.g. data to the printer on 24, status on 25), allowing one set of address decode logic to service both ports with the least significant bit selecting the function.

The address selection logic is often accompanied by some form of buffer logic to free the computer from the difficulties caused by the speed difference between peripherals and the computer. The term 'interface' is used to describe the address selection logic, the buffer logic, the connecter pins allocated for the signals and the voltages used. The interface defines the connection between a peripheral and its computer.

Serial and parallel data transmission

The simplest way to connect a peripheral and a computer is to use eight wires as shown in *Fig. 4.2*. In addition some form of strobe occurring at the centre of the data pulses to indicate 'Data present NOW' is needed. This is known as parallel transmission, and is used where high speed is required. Parallel transmission will be described in Chapter 5.

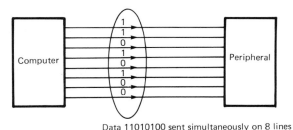

Data 11010100 sent simultaneously on 8 lines

Figure 4.2. Parallel data transmission

Usually, however, economy is more important than speed, and connecting cable is very expensive. Most peripherals connect to the computer by a single pair of wires as shown in *Fig. 4.3*, and the data is transmitted as a pulse train. Obviously, eight pulses are needed to transmit the data, plus some form of synchronising pulses to indicate where words start and finish. Serial transmission is thus approximately ten times slower than parallel transmission, but can be achieved at one eighth of the cost.

94

All microcomputers operate in parallel, and internally most peripherals operate in parallel. At both ends of a serial data link we must therefore provide parallel/serial and serial/parallel conversion logic. This is actually quite simple, and is shown in block diagram form in *Fig. 4.4*.

At both ends of the link we have a shift register and two identical clocks. Data is loaded into the transmitter shift register from the computer, and is then shifted onto the line

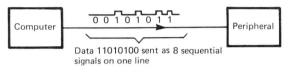

Data 11010100 sent as 8 sequential signals on one line

Figure 4.3. Serial transmission

by the clock, one bit at a time. At the receiver, the data is shifted in, one bit at a time. When all the bits have been received, the data is transferred to a buffer, and a control signal given to the peripheral to say that a word can be read from the buffer.

Although *Fig. 4.4* is drawn sending data *from* a computer *to* a peripheral, obviously identical logic would be used to send data *from* a peripheral *to* a computer.

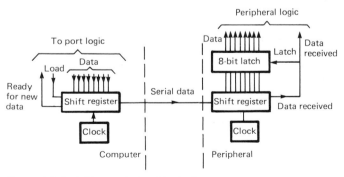

Figure 4.4. Serial transmission block diagram

Parity and error checking

All data transmission is prone to errors caused by electrical interference en route. Obviously some form of error checking is desirable. In simple peripherals this is usually done by a parity check.

One data word contains eight bits. If parity is being used, seven bits are used to carry information and one bit (called the parity bit) is used as a check. Parity can be even or odd, and quite simply the parity bit is used to ensure that the number of bits in each word is even (or odd) as selected by the system designer. An error in which one bit is altered will change the parity, which can be detected at the receiver.

Suppose we are using odd parity, and send five words down a serial link:

Transmitted	Parity	Received	Parity	
0110111	0	0110111	0	
1011100	1	1011100	1	
1011001	1	1010001	1	Error
0000111	0	1000111	0	Error
1010101	1	1010101	1	

On words 3 and 4, the parity did not match the data, and the receiver signalled an error.

Obviously parity can only detect a single error. Where errors are more frequent, or absolute security is required, more complicated error-checking codes can be used which can detect (and correct) as many errors as the designer wishes.

A common checking system is the Cyclic Redundancy Check (CRC) or sum check. Data is transmitted in blocks followed by a binary word representing the number of bits sent in the block. The receiver counts the number of bits received, and compares it with the sum check word. Usually the communication logic is arranged such that the receiver automatically requests a re-transmission of the last block when an error is detected. Although this technique slows up the data transfer, it does give a very secure communication channel.

Signals and standards

There are three common standards for serial links, although all use the same data format shown in *Fig. 4.5*. In the quiescent state, (i.e. between characters) the signal line is at a 1. The line goes to a 0 to indicate the start of a character. There then follow seven (or eight) data bits followed by the parity bit, then one (or two) 1 bits to indicate the end of the character. The 0 start bit for the next character can then be sent.

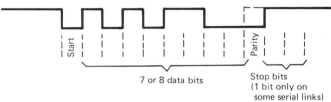

Figure 4.5. Serial transmission format

It thus takes ten or eleven bits (dependent on the system) to send one character. The speed of transmission is given in baud, which is the number of bits transmitted per second. A teletype operates at 110 baud for example, and uses two stop bits. One character will utilise 11 bits, so a teletype prints 10 characters per second. Data transfer speeds up to 9600 baud are commonly used.

The commonest serial standard is probably the 20 mA loop used initially on the ubiquitous teletype. Despite its wide use, the 20 mA loop has no official standing and no common specification. This can occasionally cause some compatibility problems.

The data in a 20 mA loop is sent as current pulses with 20 mA representing a 1 and 0 mA representing 0. In its simplest form the 20 mA loop can be represented as shown in *Fig. 4.6*, and consists of a current source, a data switch and a current sensor. Usually a transistor is used as the data switch, and an LED opto-isolator as the current sensor.

One of the complications often encountered with the current loop is the lack of formal specification for the location of the current source. A 20 mA loop can have active transmitter/passive receiver as in *Fig. 4.7a*, or a passive transmitter/active receiver as *Fig. 4.7b*.

Obviously, little communication can take place between a passive transmitter and passive receiver, so care must be taken in connecting 20 mA devices. Universal 20 mA devices have terminals allowing selection for active or passive operation. A typical connection strip for a VDU and keyboard is shown in *Fig. 4.7c*. The device has been wired for active transmission (from the keyboard) and passive reception.

Another problem often encountered is the impedance presented by the current sensor. There is no universal standard for the maximum impedance load (determined by the voltage available at the current source). Again, care should be taken in connecting supposedly compatible devices.

Despite the lack of standards, the 20 mA loop is widely used. It is particularly popular in industrial aplications where the current loop gives better noise rejection than other serial link standards.

These other two standards are known as V24 and RS232. They are almost identical, V24 being the European standard and RS232 the American standard. They are rigorously defined, and can best be explained by a simple table:

Binary state	0	1
Name	Space	Mark
Voltage	+ 3 V to + 15 V (V24)	− 3 V to − 15 V (V24)
	+ 6 V to + 15 V (RS232)	− 6 V to − 15 V (RS232)
FM (modems and telemetry)	High frequency	Low frequency
AM Modems and telemetry)	Tone off	Tone on

The specifications also cover edge speeds, impedances, etc.

In general, V24/RS232 devices are compatible. On simple serial links data is transmitted by voltages, and the standards are easy to implement. I.c.p.s are available which generate V24/RS232 signals direct from TTL signals.

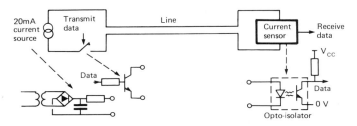

Figure 4.6. Circuits used in serial transmission

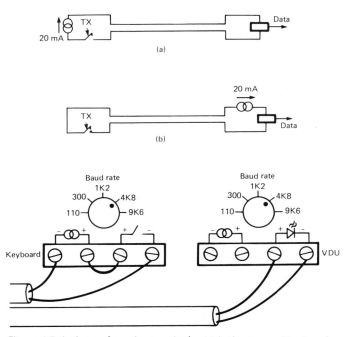

Figure 4.7. Active and passive terminals. *(a)* Active transmitter/passive receiver. *(b)* Passive transmitter/active receiver. *(c)* Typical serial link termination panel

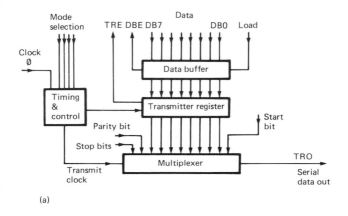

(a)

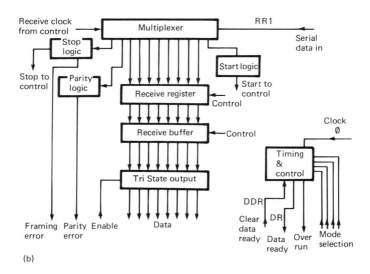

(b)

Figure 4.8. The UART. *(a)* Transmit logic. *(b)* Receive logic

UARTs

The letters UART stand for Universal Asynchronous Receiver Transmitter, and refer to an i.c.p. designed to perform both the receive and transmit logic of the serial link in *Fig. 4.4*. A block diagram of a typical UART and its connections to the outside world are shown in *Fig. 4.8*. Note that the one UART handles both transmitted and received data. *Fig. 4.8a* shows the transmitter logic and *Fig. 4.8b* the receiver logic.

Both halves of the UART have a common control logic with several mode selection inputs. These select the operating format (i.e. 5, 6, 7, 8 data bits, odd/even parity, 1 or 2 stop bits). In addition a clock signal, ϕ, is needed (usually at 16 times the data rate).

Taking the transmitter section first, data is loaded into the data buffer on DB1 to DB7. If the transmitter register is empty, the data is automatically transferred to the register. The multiplexer then selects the start bit, the data, the parity bit and the stop bits in sequence to produce the serial data TR0.

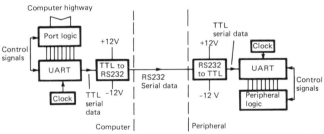

Figure 4.9. Complete RS232 serial link

The data buffer and transmitter register allow data to be loaded into the buffer whilst the previous data is being transmitted from the register. Status signals TRE, DBE indicate when the buffer or register is empty. Data transfer from buffer to register is automatic, and is done by the UART control logic.

101

Data for the receiver section arrives on RRI, and is loaded by the multiplexer into the receiver register. The parity is checked by the parity logic. When a character has been received, the status flag DR is set. The flag is cleared on DDR by the receiving device logic after the data has been read.

The receiver section incorporates many alarm flags. Parity error indicates that a parity mismatch occurred. Overrun error indicates that the DR flag was not cleared (by DDR) before a new character was received. Framing error indicates that the stop bit format was incorrect (due to noise, wrong data word length or other problems).

UARTs and the TTL/RS232 i.c.p.s described earlier can be used together to give the simple serial link shown in *Fig. 4.9*. Note that one UART is needed at each end of the link, and signal pairs are used.

Visual display units

The VDU is probably the commonest peripheral available on microcomputers, which is interesting because a decade ago VDUs were very expensive and only used on the largest mainframe computers. The dramatic fall in price has been brought about by the introduction of i.c.p.s designed specifically for VDUs, and the use of the domestic TV as the display unit.

Most VDUs display their data on a standard closed circuit TV (CCTV) monitor or domestic TV set. To understand how a VDU picture is produced it is necessary to appreciate how a television picture is displayed. It is not really practical to go into the details of a TV signal in a book of this size, but a brief description follows. Readers requiring more details of television are referred to the companion book 'Beginner's Guide to Television'.

A TV picture can be considered to be made up of many horizontal lines (625 on the British Standard) so close together that the eye cannot resolve them. These lines are drawn by an electron beam moving over the face of a TV tube, starting at the top left and moving in a zig-zag manner as shown in *Fig. 4.10* until it reaches the bottom right, whence it flies back to the top left and starts again. One complete scan takes 20 ms and is known as a frame (or a field). (This, it should be noted, is somewhat of a simplification as it ignores factors such as interlace but it is adequate for explaining the operation of a VDU.)

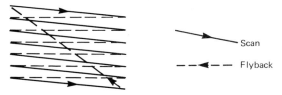

Figure 4.10. Raster scan of TV screen

As the electron beam moves its intensity is varied, which changes the brightness of the spot on the tube face. Persistence of vision causes the eye to ignore the moving spot, and we perceive a steady picture. A TV signal thus has three parts:

(a) A continuously varying luminance signal.
(b) Synchronising signals to tell the receiver when to start a new line.
(c) Synchronising signals to tell the receiver when to start a new field.

These are all combined in one composite signal as shown in *Fig. 4.11.* Video and sync signals are separated at the receiver by a level-slicing circuit, and the line and field sync pulses separated by simple RC filters.

To explain the operation of a VDU, assume one which can display 24 rows of characters, each row containing 72 characters. (We will refer to character rows to avoid confusion with TV lines.) To store these characters a store of $72 \times 24 \times 1$ bytes will be needed, since each character is held as an eight-bit word. It is convenient to consider this store as being arranged in the same manner as the display, with an X address determining the character position in a row, and a Y address determining the row. The location 47, 15 thus refers to the 47th character on the 15th row.

The VDU display consists of 72 × 24 character cells, each cell displaying one character. Each cell is broken down into a matrix of dots, common arrangements being 7 × 10, 7 × 9, and 5 × 7. Each line of the matrix corresponds to one TV line (for larger characters several TV lines could be used for each

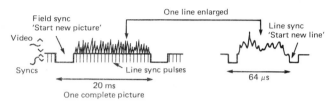

Figure 4.11. Composite video signal (simplified and not to scale).

cell line, but a 1:1 relationship is assumed here for simplicity). *Fig. 4.12* shows a 7 × 9 matrix, and the dot pattern for the letter A.

A character row will be displayed one TV line at a time, so the TV signal will consist of:

Row 1 line 1 character 1; .... line 1 character 72
        line 2 character 2; .... line 2 character 72

        line 9 character 1; .... line 9 character 72
Row 2 line 1 character 1;
and so on, for all 24 rows.

The characters in the VDU store are converted to their dot patterns by a special ROM called a character generator. It

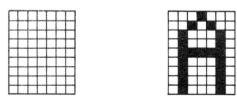

Figure 4.12. 7 × 9 dot matrix

might be thought that this would have an eight-bit input and 63 outputs for the 7 × 9 elements of the matrix. However, as the characters are drawn one line at a time, all that is required from the ROM is the data for the current line.

A typical ROM is shown in *Fig. 4.13*. There are two inputs: an eight-bit data input representing the character required, and a four-bit input telling the ROM which line we are on. The seven outputs give the seven dots for the selected line of the specified character.

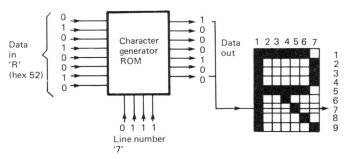

Figure 4.13. Character generator ROM

Suppose the letter R is being displayed and the seventh line is being drawn. The inputs are the data for R (01010010 in binary, 52 in hex) and the line number, 7, in binary (0111). The ROM output is 1000100, which is the dot pattern for the seventh line of the letter R.

A typical character generator ROM is the MCM 6576, whose character set is shown in *Fig. 4.14*.

The seven dot outputs from the character generator ROM need to be serialised before they can be used as a video signal. This is achieved by loading them into a shift register, and shifting them out one bit at a time as shown in *Fig. 4.15*. (see parallel to serial conversion above).

All that remains now is to bring the characters from the store to the ROM at the correct time. This is done by the straightforward, if somewhat lengthy, timing chain of *Fig. 4.16*.

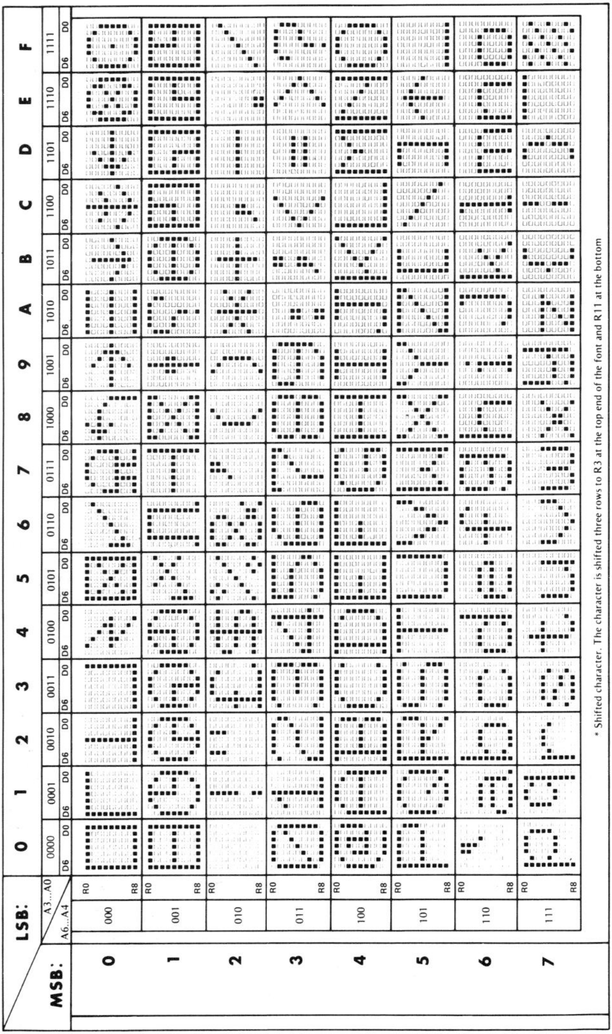

Figure 4.14. Typical character generator ROM contents

* Shifted character. The character is shifted three rows to R3 at the top end of the font and R11 at the bottom

The operation starts with a clock running at the bit rate of the matrix. This clocks the ROM output shift register and a divide-by-seven counter. Since a character comprises seven dots per line, the X counter will be stepped every seven dots, and therefore holds the current row position. It can thus be used directly as the X store address.

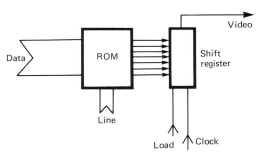

Figure 4.15. Conversion of ROM output to video

Each character occupies nine TV lines, so the X counter is followed by a divide-by-nine counter, whose four-bit output is used as the line number for the character generator ROM. When all nine TV lines have been drawn, we start a new character row by stepping the Y counter which holds the Y address for the data store.

When all lines of all rows have been drawn, all counters go back to zero and the whole operation is repeated for the next TV field. With the X and Y addresses defined in time, the store gives the correct data to the ROM at the correct time, and the output of the shift register will be the VDU video signals.

The sync pulses are generated by an SPG (sync pulse generator) i.c.p., and combined with the video to give a composite CCTV signal suitable for a CCTV monitor. If the signal is being used with a domestic TV, the CCTV signal will be modulated on to a UHF carrier to simulate the TV signal received by an aerial.

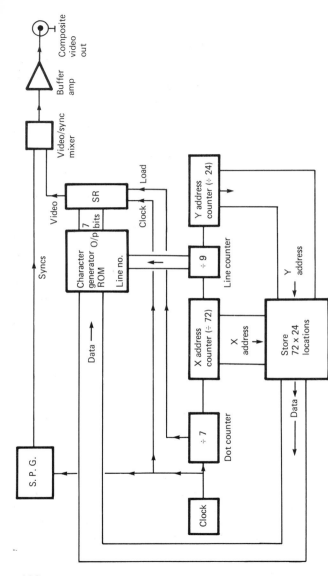

Figure 4.16. Block diagraM OF VDU

Loading the store

We have seen how we can convert the data in an X, Y addressed store into a VDU display. To be of any use, however, the data must be loaded into the store in the first place. The data store must obviously be a read/write random access store similar to a computer store. Data arrives from the computer, probably along a serial link, and is loaded into the store in one of two ways.

The first, and simplest, is called 'scroll mode'. In this operating mode the programmer does not need to worry about the position of the data on the screen. Incoming data is written along the bottom row of the VDU (row 24), and when a 'new row' control signal is received, all VDU rows move up one. Row 1 (the top row) is lost. The VDU thus resembles a sheet of paper scrolling up from a typewriter.

Scroll mode is easy to use, but has many limitations. It cannot be used to display fast changing data, or to construct mimic diagrams. Greater versatility is given by the operating mode called 'page mode'.

In page mode, a single character can be written in any position on the screen. The current writing location is defined by the XY co-ordinates of a cursor, control codes being used to move the cursor. The cursor control codes commonly used are:

Cursor home (X = Y = O, top left)
Cursor up (decrement Y)
Cursor down (increment Y)
Cursor left (decrement X)
Cursor right (increment X)
Start row (X = O, Y unchanged)
New row (X = O, increment Y)

In the absence of a control code, the cursor moves one position to the right after each character is loaded.

With page mode, static displays can be drawn, and individual data words can be changed without affecting the rest of the screen. Obviously this is achieved at the expense of some complication for the programmer who must, at all times, know where the VDU cursor is located.

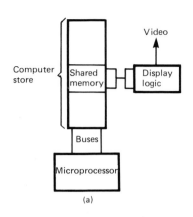

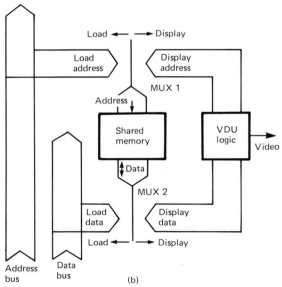

Figure 4.17. (a) Memory mapped VDU. (b) Detailed diagram of memory mapped VDU

Memory mapped VDUs

If the VDU is an integral part of a microcomputer, a simple technique can be used. The VDU data store can be constructed as part of the computer RAM as shown in *Fig. 4.17a*, giving the computer full access to every VDU location. Data for the VDU is put into the store by a load (move) instruction, and the data can be read, or even used in calculations, at any time.

The arrangement is shown in more detail in *Fig. 4.17b*. The VDU store can be connected either to the VDU display logic or the computer, and is switched by two multiplexers. Normally the store is connected to the VDU logic, but is briefly switched over when the computer requires access.

Memory mapped VDUs are inherently a form of page mode and are very versatile. Unfortunately the address bus and data bus in a microcomputer can only be a few tens of centimetres in length, so a memory mapped VDU can only be implemented as an integral part of a computer.

VDU variations

VDU graphics are widely used for mimic diagrams and games. Additional non-alphanumeric characters, such as those in *Fig. 4.18*, are provided by a graphics ROM. Character

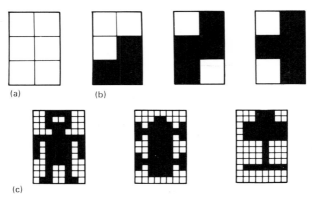

(a)   (b)

(c)

Figure 4.18. Graphics and gaming characters. *(a)* Graphics cell. *(b)* Typical graphics characters. *(c)* Gaming characters

111

cells for graphics characters are taller than those used for text to bridge the gap between rows. Large solid areas can then be drawn. This is sometimes referred to as low-resolution graphics.

High-resolution graphics allow the programmer to address individual dots on the screen. A typical high-resolution VDU would allow addressing of 600 × 400 individual dots called pixels. Programming for high-resolution graphics is obviously complex, but the results are impressive, *Fig. 4.19* being typical. Often, the programmer can request a circle radius R units centred on point X, Y or a line joining X1, Y1 to X2, Y2,

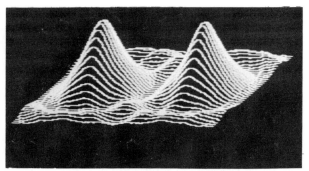

Figure 4.19. High resolution graphics (Photo: Strathand)

leaving the machine itself to work out which points to illuminate. High-resolution machines incorporate functions such as CIRCLE and PLOT in the BASIC instruction set.

Colour adds a new dimension to VDU displays. A colour TV uses three colours (red, green, blue), which can be combined to give eight colours: red, green, blue, yellow, cyan, magenta, white, black. These eight colours can be represented by three bits, so we need six bits to define character colour and background colour (e.g. a red letter G on a green background). Sometimes a seventh bit is used to denote a flashing character.

The simplest way to program a colour VDU is to use control codes to define colour changes. A control code appears as a blank on the screen, so colours can only be changed at spaces between words or at gaps in graphics; this is sometimes called Teletext graphics. Greater versatility is obtained by using a longer data word to specify foreground and background colour individually for each character. In BASIC, the words INK (for foreground colour) and PAPER (for background colour) are often used.

Printers

Most of the microcomputers designed for home or small business use come equipped with a VDU in one form or another, so a printer is probably the first peripheral considered by most users. A printer allows permanent copies to be kept of programs and results, and is really essential for any commercial installation.

Figure 4.20. Golfball print head

Printers can be roughly classified into four types; teleprinters, matrix, daisywheel and line printers. Printers based on conventional typewriter mechanisms are almost unknown with computers because they are inherently slow.

The term teleprinter covers devices such as the ubiquitous Teletype 33 and the IBM golfball, which use a print system similar to *Fig. 4.20.* The characters are embossed on a small drum. To print a character the drum is rotated and elevated

113

until the character is in the print position. The drum is then locked and brought into contact with the paper.

The operation of teleprinters is a triumph of mechanical ingenuity, but because they rely on solenoids and complex linkages they are also slow (10 characters per second) and somewhat unreliable. Teleprinters are very popular with amateur computer users as they are cheaply and easily obtained on the second-hand market.

Most new computer installations nowadays use some form of matrix printer. The operating principle of a matrix printer is shown on *Fig. 4.21*. A small, movable type-head has a vertical column of seven (in some nine) needles driven by solenoids. As the type head moves across the page the pins are energised to build the character up on a matrix similar to those used for VDUs in the previous section. The decoding to determine which solenoids are to be energised is done by a character generator ROM.

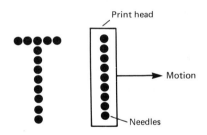

Figure 4.21. The matrix printer

Matrix printers are very fast (up to 300 plus characters per second) and sufficiently quiet to be used in an office environment (teleprinters are incredibly noisy and are usually housed in soundproof cabinets). The only moving parts are the solenoids, print head and ribbon transport, making matrix printers very reliable. The only real disadvantage is the print quality. On most matrix printers the dot pattern can be readily seen, which makes them unsuitable for word processor and similar applications. Diagonal lines on the letters N and Y are particularly poor.

114

Daisywheel printers are used where good print quality is required. The characters are embossed on the petals of a daisy-shaped wheel similar to *Fig. 4.22*. The wheel is spun at high speed, and the wheel position is detected by a suitable sensor. When the selected character comes to the print position the print hammer solenoid is energised.

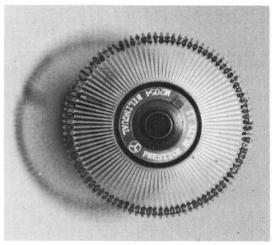

Figure 4.22. A daisywheel print head

The print quality from a daisywheel printer is as good as any office typewriter, making daisywheels mandatory for word processors. The print speed (around 50 characters per second) is slower than a matrix printer, but in most applications where daisywheels are used this is not important. A big advantage of the daisywheel printer is the ease with which the daisywheel itself can be changed, allowing many different typefaces to be used on the same printer.

Line printers are used for commercial installations and are really rather rare on microcomputers. There are three basic types (drum, chain and comb) but all work in a similar manner by printing a complete line of text at once. All are large, expensive but very fast (up to 300 lines per minute).

Observations on printers

It does not follow that a printer quoted at, say, 120 characters per second will print text at 120 characters per second. The paper advance and carriage return are usually slow operations, so the actual printing speed will depend on the text line length. A useful feature which obviates the time consuming carriage return is bidirectional printing where the print head goes left to right on one line, and right to left on the next. Bidirectional printing can be a nuisance, however, on short lines since the printer always prints a full line, padding out with spaces to the end of the line.

Printers connect to the computer via serial interfaces or parallel interfaces (the operation of parallel interfaces is described in the next chapter). There is no real standard for parallel printers, but the interface developed for Centronics printers is widely used by other manufacturers. Many printers incorporate a character store to allow the computer to send blocks of text at a speed well in excess of the print speed. Bidirectional and line printers must have a store capable of holding at least one complete line.

Most printers use inked ribbon similar to those on typewriters (loading a new ribbon on some can resemble a mechanical aptitude test) but other print schemes are in use. Electro-sensitive and heat-sensitive printers use a matrix head identical to those described earlier, but are loaded with special paper which discolours on the application of, respectively, an electric potential or heat from the pins. The main advantage of these printers is the high speed and almost spookily silent operation. They do suffer from the serious disadvantage that special (and hence expensive) paper is required.

Many cheap matrix printers economise by not providing descenders on letters such as f, g, y, z. These letters are shifted up to produce odd-looking text with words such as PaYin8. More expensive printers will have proper descenders, and often will reproduce graphic symbols. In general it should be assumed that matrix printers not specifically mentioning full descenders will not have them.

There are two types of paper feed found on printers; sprocket feed and friction feed. Sprocket feed uses sprocket holes in the paper edges to grip the paper, and is mandatory for continuous stationery printing (such as payslips and invoices) where precise registration of the text is needed. Sprocket feed is rather unsightly for other applications however.

Friction-feed printers rely on the pressure between the platen roll and the paper. Friction feed can be used with continuous stationery, but registration can be a problem and often the paper has the annoying habit of creeping to one side. The major advantage of friction-feed printers, though, is their ability to take single sheets of paper.

Printers of all types are expensive items, and it is by no means unusual for a printer to cost more than the computer to which it is attached. Unfortunately printers are necessary for any serious computer installations, so it can only be hoped that large scale production will lead to price reductions in the not-too-distant future.

Keyboards

Keyboards allow data to be typed directly into a computer. Usually a keyboard is used in conjunction with some output peripheral such as a printer or VDU.

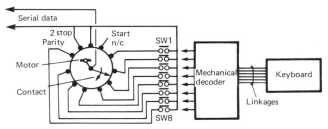

Figure 4.23. Electromechanical keyboard

Mechanical keyboards are often used with teleprinters, and are an amazing collection of linkages, cams and levers, although in essence they follow the block diagram of *Fig. 4.23*. When a key is depressed, a mechanical decoder produces the seven-bit ASCII coding plus parity bit on SW1 –SW8. At the same time the clutch is made between the rotary switch (called a distributor) and the motor. As the switch rotates, the start bit, data bits, parity bits and stop bits are transmitted. When the switch comes back to the park position the clutch opens again. Serial data is thus transmitted on to the line from the keyboard.

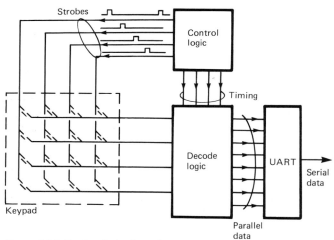

Figure 4.24. Electronic keyboard

Electronic keyboards are usually arranged on a matrix similar to *Fig. 4.24*. The keys close a contact (often a reed relay or Hall-effect switch) which connects one column of the matrix to one row. The columns are strobed in turn by the control logic, and the rows read by the decoding logic. If, for example, row 3 is energised when column 2 is strobed, key R has been pressed. The strobes on the columns operate continuously giving far higher typing speeds than any mechanical method.

The decoder produces a parallel ASCII-coded output which can be used directly with parallel I/O, or used with a UART to give a serial output.

Electronic keyboards can suffer from keybounce, either in the switches themselves or from hesitant fingers. Usually the decoder will incorporate some form of filter to remove bounce.

Keyboards can have many useful options. A particularly useful feature is multiple key rollover which allows a key to be detected before the previous key is released. Key repeat is another useful feature, repeating a character as long as a key is pressed.

Cassette interfaces

Most microcomputers have volatile stores, and therefore require some way of storing programs and data for later use. Although disc systems can be used, they are relatively expensive. The domestic cassette recorder is used on many microcomputers as a cheap, but surprisingly effective, alternative to discs. With care, data transfer rates of over 2000 baud can be achieved, although 300 baud is more typical.

There are two ways or recording data on cassettes, both using tones. The first uses a tone burst to represent a 1, and the absence of a tone to represent a 0 (a form of amplitude modulation). The second (and more common) method uses two tones, one to represent a 1, and the other to represent a 0 (a form of frequency modulation).

In 1975, a symposium of amateur computer enthusiasts at Kansas City discussed cassette systems and proposed a standard of 1200 Hz for a 0 and 2400 Hz for a 1. This became known as the Kansas City standard and is as nearly an industry standard. (Also known as CUTS for Computer Users' Tape System.)

It does not follow, however, that 'Kansas City' tapes are interchangeable between different computers. There is little trouble between similar makes of computer (e.g. PET to PET, or TRS-80 to TRS-80) but there is no compatibility between different makes due to inherent differences in the way the resident software has been written.

Cassette interfaces work very well, and because the record and playback circuits consist of a UART and a handful of chips they are very cheap. An expensive tape recorder is not necessary (or even desirable). The author was recently involved in evaluating recorders for use with several industrial computer systems. The best (and most consistent) results were obtained with the cheapest recorders from a local discount store!

Large mainframe computers also use magnetic tapes to store data. The operating principles of these tape systems are much more complex than the simple microcomputer cassette interface and allow data transfers at considerably higher speeds. These commercial tape units are rarely encountered with microcomputers.

Discs

Although cheap, cassette storage has several disadvantages. The first is speed, as a cassette can take minutes to load a 16K program. The second, and more basic, problem is the lack of control that the computer has over the cassette fast forward, rewind and play buttons. It is not usually possible to put a cassette into the player, and tell the computer to find and load the data file 'FRED'. At best the computer can work its way through all the data on the tape until it finds FRED and then load it. This operation could take tens of minutes without a human being to wind the tape to the right area.

Where large amounts of data are to be processed, access times need to be measured in milliseconds rather than minutes, so some faster form of bulk storage is obviously required. This is usually provided by magnetic discs.

The elements of a disc system are shown on *Fig. 4.25*. A disc, coated with magnetic material, is rotated at high speed under a movable record/playback head. The data is recorded on concentric tracks (unlike a gramophone record which uses a spiral). Each track is further divided into sectors, so a particular block of data is identified by a sector on a track. Access time is determined by the rotational speed of the disc and the head-positioning time.

Rigid metal discs are used on minicomputer systems. These discs can store around 700 Megabytes of data with an access time of 50 ms. To prevent the head grinding the disc surface a technique known as a 'flying head' is used. As the disc rotates, a thin layer of air is dragged round, which is used to keep the head flying close to the surface without actually touching it.

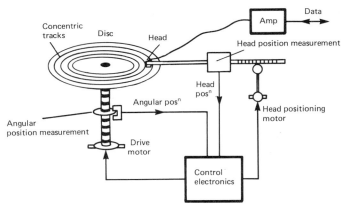

Figure 4.25. Elements of a disc system

A rigid disc drive can hold vast amounts of data, and is really unnecessary for an average microcomputer. They are also very expensive. A cheaper alternative, the floppy disc (or diskette) has been developed for the microcomputer market.

A floppy disc (shown on *Fig. 4.26*) is a thin, plastic magnetic disc about the size of a 45 r.p.m. record, contained in a protective paper envelope. The head contacts the disc in the rectangular slot. Unlike a rigid disc system, the record/ playback head actually touches the disc surface. To prevent excessive wear the floppy disc revolves considerably slower than its rigid relations. A typical floppy rotates at 360 r.p.m., a typical rigid disc at 2400 r.p.m. Access times are increased correspondingly, 200 ms being quoted for most floppies.

Sectors on floppy discs can be determined either by hardware (known as hard sectors) or by software (known as soft sector). Hard-sector discs use small holes in the disc surface which are sensed by a photocell to identify sectors.

Figure 4.26. A floppy disc

Common standards are 10 or 16 holes per rotation. Soft-sector discs have only one hole per rotation to identify a datum position. Sectors are then identified by the program. Soft-sector discs are more versatile at the expense of program complexity.

A standard format often encountered is known as IBM-compatible. This utilises 73 data tracks, each track having 26 sectors, and each sector capable of holding 64 words. This gives a storage capacity of 121 472 words on a single disc (about one sixtieth of the capacity of a rigid disc).

Data transfer between discs and the computer involves fairly complex hardware and software techniques. The hardware used (DMA) is described below. The software problems

122

are largely eliminated (for the user at least) by Disc Operating Systems (DOS). Each computer and disc manufacturer has his own operating system, and the only system which is really independent is CP/M (for console processor and monitor.)

When data is not being transferred the head is lifted off the disc to reduce wear. Head and disc life are therefore determined by use, and floppies are not really suitable for applications where data is being continually transferred between discs and the microcomputer.

With both rigid and floppy disc systems, a certain amount of care is needed when handling or storing the discs. Magnetic fields (from TV monitors or power supplies) can corrupt the data, and dust can cause severe damage to head and disc surfaces. A 'no smoking' rule should be adopted when working with discs.

A recent development is the Winchester disc drive which combines some of the advantages of both rigid and floppy discs in one system. In a Winchester disc, the drive and head form a totally self-contained unit, with its own closed-loop air system. Because the disc and its hardware are manufactured together, far tighter manufacturing tolerances are possible, giving higher data density. Winchester discs lie between floppy and rigid discs in access time, density and cost. The Winchester disc system is particularly well suited for industrial applications where clean environments are difficult to provide.

Direct memory access (DMA)

It is technically feasible to connect a disc system to a computer via a serial or parallel I/O port, but this would present many problems. Data is transferred to and from discs in large blocks and, at the fastest transfer speed of 9600 baud, it would take many seconds to transfer a reasonable size data block. More important, though, each word would have to be transferred by the computer program, utilising the CPU the whole time the transfer was in progress. If a disc system is not to become a bottleneck, some alternative method of controlling the transfer is needed.

An operating system is provided with the stringy floppy to allow files to be opened, loaded, read and modified in a manner similar to disc operating systems. To the user the stringy floppy appears as a somewhat slow disc drive.

Modems

Microcomputers often operate peripherals that are located a considerable distance away. The easiest way to do this is to transmit the data over existing telephone cables. The data is converted into tones similar to those used on a cassette interface, and the tones transmitted over the telephone lines. At the peripheral the tones are converted back to pulses. With good quality cables, transmission rates up to 2400 baud are possible but lower rates are more common.

The circuit at each end which converts data to tones and back again is known as a Modem (for modulator/demodulator). The telephone authorities are understandably concerned about equipment being connected on to their lines, and lay down very strict regulations to prevent crosstalk to other users and possible hazards to their engineers who work on live cables. In general, only authorized equipment is allowed to be connected to public lines. No such restrictions apply to private lines.

Approved modems are usually only available on rental, but an interesting alternative not requiring approval is an acoustic coupler. This consists of a peculiar-looking moulding into which a telephone handset is placed. The unit contains a microphone and speaker which are located respectively beneath the telephone earpiece and mouthpiece. On transmit, the unit converts the data into tones which pass via the mouthpiece on to the line. On receive, the incoming tones are picked up from the earpiece by the microphone, and demodulated to produce data again. Because no direct electrical connection is necessary, acoustic couplers do not require approval. They can also be used from any telephone, which could be useful in some circumstances.

5

The microcomputer in control

The microcomputer is particularly well suited for control of other equipment. The topic of control covers a wide spectrum from control of large industrial processes, through data logging and laboratory experiments, to the humble control of a domestic washing machine or kitchen oven.

All these uses require the microcomputer to communicate with the outside world, but not in alphanumeric symbols. Data in control applications is the closing of limit switches, the energising of relays, the reading of variables such as temperature, pressure etc. In most control schemes, this communication takes place via parallel ports.

Parallel input/output

Parallel I/O is simpler than the serial I/O described in the previous chapter. In its basic form, it consists of the simple circuit of *Fig. 5.1* which shows a simple memory mapped parallel output port. When the port address is placed on the address bus by the CPU, the port address decode logic strobes the clock line on the eight D-type flip-flops, gating the data from the data bus to the outside world.

Fig. 5.1b shows a simple parallel input port. When the port is addressed, data is strobed from the outside world to the data bus for use by the CPU. TriState buffers are used to connect to the bus.

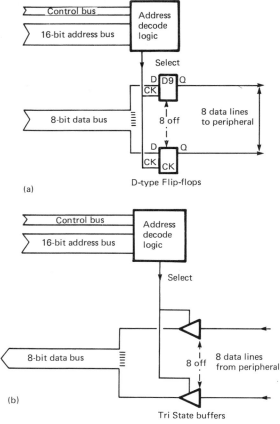

(a)

D-type Flip-flops

(b)

Tri State buffers

Figure 5.1. Parallel I/O ports. *(a)* Simple output port. *(b)* Simple input port

Both the circuits shown in *Fig. 5.1* are very easy to construct, with chips such as the Intel 8212 containing an eight-bit latched buffer and TriState outputs specifically for parallel I/O. In most applications, though, a technique known as 'handshaking' is used to check that the data transfer has been achieved.

128

Handshaking requires two additional lines between an I/O port and the outside world, along with the eight data lines. A handshake output port is shown in *Fig. 5.2a* with the timing in *Fig. 5.2b*.

At time A, the computer changes the data from the port. After a short delay to allow the lines to settle, the 'ready' line is energised at time B. This informs the peripheral device that

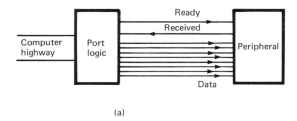

(a)

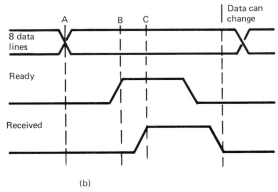

(b)

Figure 5.2. Output port with handshake. *(a)* Handshake signals. *(b)* Timing

stable data is present, and the data can be loaded into the peripheral logic. When the peripheral has received the data, the peripheral signals via the 'data received' line at time C. When the port logic receives this signal, the ready line is cleared for the next transfer.

A handshake input works in a similar manner, except the transfer is usually initiated by a peripheral device. *Fig. 5.3a* shows a typical scheme, with the timing in *Fig. 5.3b*.

When the input buffer is empty, the 'ready for data' line is at a 1. The peripheral device initiates the sequence by presenting data to the port and signalling 'data present'. The

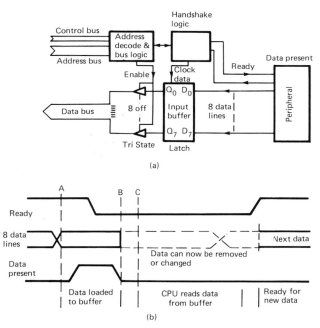

Figure 5.3. Input port with handshake. *(a)* Handshake logic. *(b)* Timing

port logic strobes the data into the buffer, and puts the ready line to a 0 to indicate to the peripheral that the data has been received, but has not yet been read by the CPU. When the peripheral sees the ready line go to a 0, the data present signal, and the data itself, are removed (time B).

130

As yet, the CPU has not been involved, and the data has yet to be brought from the input buffer. Commonly the port control will interrupt the CPU (see below) or the input buffer will simply be read at regular intervals.

The input buffer is read by the CPU at time C by addressing the port as described earlier for the simpler *Fig. 5.1b*. When the data has been read from the input buffer, the port control logic clears the input buffer and puts the ready line to a 1 again to indicate to the peripheral that the data has been read by the CPU. The port is now available to receive a new data word from the peripheral.

Parallel I/O i.c.p.s

Although it is possible to construct parallel I/O ports with discrete logic, it is easier to use the special i.c.p.s designed specifically to implement the control of the handshake, data, etc. in *Figs. 5.2.* and *5.3*. These chips are known variously as PIO (parallel input/output), PIA (peripheral interface adapter), or PPI (programmable peripheral interface).

Despite the different names given to these chips, the operating principles are basically similar. There are slight differences, so we shall look upon the Zilog Z-80 PIO as being typical. Other devices (from Intel, Motorola, and other manufacturers) are very similar.

The PIO chip can handle two totally separate eight-bit ports, known as A and B. The ports can be configured in any one of four modes:

    i. Input. The eight bits are treated as inputs, with full handshake.

    ii. Output. The eight bits are treated as outputs, with full handshake.

    iii. Bidirectional. The eight bits can be treated as input or output, and will respond to CPU IN or OUT instructions. Full handshake in both directions is provided.

    iv. Control. Each bit in the eight-bit word can be specified as an input or an output, and responds to CPU IN or OUT instructions. No handshaking is used.

The internal architecture is shown in *Fig. 5.4*. The chip is selected by the CE input (chip enable) which is driven from the address decode. In addition an A/B select input is provided. This determines whether the CPU accesses the A or B port. Finally, we have a control/data pin. Control outputs are used to select which of the four operating modes is to be used, and should not be confused with the control operating mode outlined in iv. above.

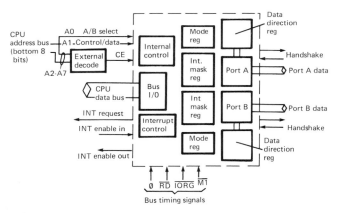

Figure 5.4. Z-80 PIO architecture

Normally, the A/B select is connected directly to line 0 of the address highway, and the control/data to bit 1 as shown. The PIO chip will then have four addresses. Suppose the address decode responds to address 4. We should then have:

Address 4	A Data
5	B Data
6	A Control Word
7	B Control Word

An operating mode is selected by making an output to the control address. In hex, the modes are selected by the following data:

Input	4F
Output	0F
Bidirectional	8F
Control	FF

When the control mode has been selected, a further output to the control address is required to specify which bits in the port are to be inputs and which are outputs. This is done simply by putting a 1 into the control word where an input bit is needed. If we have bits 1, 3 and 4 as inputs, the control word would be 00011010 or 1A in hex. This pattern is stored in the Data Direction Register (DDR) as shown in *Fig. 5.4*.

With the operating mode set, data can now be output or input to both ports on addresses 4 or 5. The handshake signals operate as before, but all the sequencing is handled by the PIO chip itself.

Interrupts

An industrial control system with many inputs can be handled in two ways. The first, and least efficient, method is called 'polling'. In essence, a computer using a polling system simply examines all inputs at regular intervals (say twice per second) and takes action according to the inputs it finds present.

Polling is a very inefficient use of CPU time. An input which occurs once a year (e.g. low oil level in a hydraulic system) still has to be examined twice a second if a fast response is required. Programming for polling can also be complex, as the programmer has to ensure that the input scan is maintained under all conceivable circumstances.

Inputs are more commonly handled by a technique known as 'interrupts'. When a device requires the attention of the CPU, it sends a signal which causes the CPU to complete its current instruction, then attend to the needs of the initiating device. Apart from being very fast, this technique does not tie the computer up in repetitive polling of all inputs.

Usually a hierarchy of interrupt priorities is established according to the needs of the plant being controlled. A typical priority would be:

Mundane (e.g. printer paper low)
Informative (e.g. motor tripped)
Operational (e.g. normal plant inputs, operators' controls)
Plant danger (e.g. oil level low, bearings over temperature)
Personnel danger (e.g. molten steel breakout, boiler water level low)

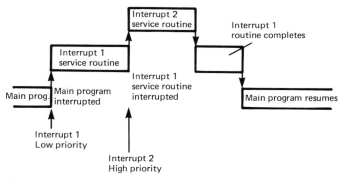

Figure 5.5. Handling interrupts

A computer servicing a high-priority interrupt would ignore lower levels until it was safe to do so. Similarly, a computer servicing an interrupt would interrupt that operation if a more urgent interrupt occurred. A typical sequence of interrupt handling is shown in *Fig. 5.5.*

This hierarchy is easily established by a daisy-chain principle. Each PIO has an input 'interrupt disable' and an output 'interrupt in progress'. The latter signal is present if the PIO chip is generating an interrupt, or the disable signal is present. If a series of PIOs are daisy-chained as in *Fig. 5.6,* any PIO-generated interrupt will cause an interrupt request to be signalled to the CPU. In *Fig. 5.6* PIO 4 is generating an interrupt, and interrupts from PIOs 1 to 3 are inhibited. PIO 4 is thus a higher priority than PIOs 1 to 3.

If PIO 5 now generated an interrupt, the interrupts from PIOs 1 to 4 would be inhibited (including the one being dealt with from PIO 4) and a new interrupt request would be presented to the CPU. The CPU would suspend the sequence triggered by PIO 4 and deal with PIO 5.

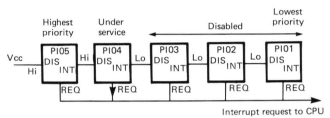

Figure 5.6. Daisy-chaining of interrupts

The priority of the interrupts therefore increases to the left of *Fig. 5.6*. Daisy-chaining of interrupt requests is a simple way of determining the priority hierarchy.

In general, all bits on one port will generate an interrupt of the same priority since only one interrupt signal is provided from each port. Internally, though, a mask register is included in the PIO to allow interrupts to be allowed only from particular bits in the byte. This register is loaded from the CPU, and its contents can be altered according to circumstances. In addition, a mode register is provided to specify whether an interrupt is generated on a 1 to 0, or a 0 to 1, transition.

When the CPU receives an interrupt request, the current instruction is completed, and the instruction counter pushed on to the stack as described earlier for subroutines. The CPU must now identify the interrupting device and jump to the routine for handling it. Different microprocessors handle interrupts in different ways, but a description of the methods used by the 8080 and Z-80 will show two different approaches and illustrate the principles.

An interrupting device on an 8080 system is connected to the CPU via an interrupt controller which determines the priority in a similar manner to daisy-chains (see *Fig. 5.7.*). When an interrupt occurs, the controller notifies the CPU, then, when the current instruction has been completed and the instruction counter pushed on to the stack, the controller forces an instruction on to the data bus. This will normally be a jump instruction to the routine servicing the interrupting peripheral.

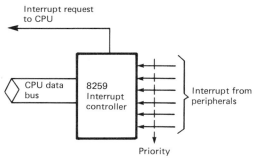

Figure 5.7. The 8259 interrupt controller

Obviously the controller must store a jump instruction for each interrupting device. These are loaded to registers in the controller by the CPU, usually by treating the register as memory mapped I/O.

The Z-80 operates in a somewhat different manner by allocating part of the store to hold addresses of servicing routines. The most significant byte of this area is loaded to the I register by the CPU. The least significant byte is held in a register in the PIO chip and is forced on to the data bus by the PIO chip. This byte is known as the vector.

The operation is a little involved, so assume that the servicing routine addresses are held in location 0C00 onwards. The I register will be loaded with 0C. An interrupt occurs at a PIO, whose vector register contains 60. The address of the servicing routine is held in 0C60 (low byte) and 0C61 (high byte). Assume 0C60 contains F7 and 0C61 contains

42. The servicing routine starts at 42F7 and the CPU will jump to that address.

The keys to this method are the I register and the vector register in each PIO. These are loaded by the CPU before the main program is executed.

The Z-80 and the 8080 allow the interrupting device to indicate the address of the servicing routine. Other methods are used in different machines. On some, the CPU is simply informed that an interrupt has occurred. This causes the CPU to jump to a servicing routine which polls all peripherals to see which initiated the interrupt. Having established the origin of the interrupt, the CPU jumps to the appropriate routine.

Whatever method is used, however, the operation can be summarised:

     i. Interrupt occurs. CPU completes current instruction.

     ii. Instruction counter pushed on to stack.

     iii. CPU identifies interrupting device, and jumps to servicing routine.

     iv. Servicing routine obeyed.

     v. Routine terminates with a Return from Interrupt instruction.

     vi. Instruction counter pulled from stack, main program resumes.

During stage iv. the servicing routine can itself be interrupted by a higher priority device.

We have so far assumed that interrupts are generated by inputs. Most PIO chips also have facilities to generate an interrupt on the successful completion of an output, (point C on *Fig. 5.2b*). This allows the CPU to initiate an output, then proceed with other work. When the peripheral has completed the output transaction the interrupt will signal to the CPU that further data can be sent.

Interrupts can also be generated by serial devices, although the interrupt signalling requires additional cable and the identification of the interrupting device is more difficult.

All CPUs can enable and disable interrupts by program, either internally within the CPU or by disabling specific specific ports. This gives the programmer considerable flexibility in dealing with outside events.

Handling interrupts is probably one of the more complex programming tasks, and is complicated further by the different techniques used by different microprocessor manufacturers. Interrupts are, however, the only way of communicating successfully with the real world outside.

Requirements for control

Any control scheme, be it relay, electronic or computer, can be drawn as in *Fig. 5.8*. On the left we have inputs, which will include operator controls, limit switches, and analog readings such as temperature, pressure, flow, or speed. On the right we have outputs, including relays, motor contactors,

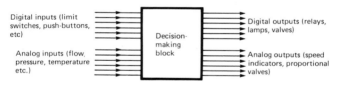

Figure 5.8. Universal control scheme

hydraulic valves and analog variables for indicators, chart recorders, speed references, etc. Linking the input and outputs is a decision-making block which drives the outputs according to the conditions observed on the inputs. This decision-making block can be implemented in many ways, but of particular interest to us is the use of a control microcomputer.

Before we can deal with the control microcomputer, we must first deal with our four forms of communications with the outside world.

Digital inputs

An eight-bit word can convey information on the state of eight contacts. These contacts must be monitored in the presence of electrical interference which could not only cause false indications but, under extreme conditions, could cause the computer to misbehave. In addition, precautions should be taken to prevent external faults, such as cable damage, introducing high voltages into the computer.

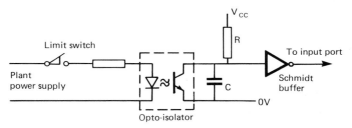

Figure 5.9. Opto-isolated input

These problems are overcome by a technique known as opto-isolation shown on *Fig. 5.9*. The plant-side contacts are connected to their own power supply, and there is no direct electrical connection between the plant and the computer. When a contact makes, its light-emitting diode lights, turning on the companion phototransistor which is connected to the input PIO. Simple RC filtering is used to overcome switch bounce.

The absence of any direct connection and the relatively low circuit impedance give excellent noise rejection. Opto-isolators will stand in excess of 600 volts between the input LED and output phototransistor. With normal supply voltages of 240 or 440 volts, no conceivable external fault can cause damage to the computer itself.

Digital outputs

The arguments for opto-isolation as outlined above apply equally to digital outputs, but there is another potential problem. Most digital outputs will switch some heavy-current device (e.g. solenoids, relays, and in-rush current on lamps). If the return current shares any paths with the logic, noise problems will amost certainly ensue.

A typical opto-isolated output, shown on *Fig. 5.10*, will have its own separate power supply. Often a common supply

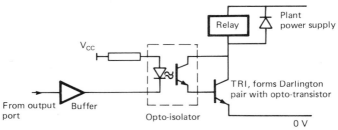

Figure 5.10. Opto-isolated output

will be used for opto-isolated inputs and outputs. If a DC supply is being used, Darlington transistors can be used to give high current gain.

AC outputs can be switched directly by the use of triacs and AC solid state relays (SSRs) can be easily obtained which will switch a 15 amp load from a logic level. These incorporate opto-isolation and zero-crossing logic to minimise mains-borne interference.

Analog outputs
Analog outputs will be described before inputs because the basic analog output building block is used to construct an analog input device. An eight-bit word can represent a number in the range 0 to 255 (or -128 to $+127$ if two's complement arithmetic is used). This represents a resolution of about 0.5 per cent which is adequate for most applications.

An analog output device will convert an eight-bit binary word to a voltage. For example, it could produce a voltage in the range 0 to 2.55 volts in 0.01 volt steps. The binary number:

10110101

would thus give 1.81 volts out of the device.

An analog output block is known as a DAC (for Digital to Analog Converter) and is usually based on the R-2R resistor chain of *Fig. 5.11*. Analysis shows that the output voltage is given by the binary pattern on the switches SW1–SW8. The switches are usually implemented by FETs. Although DACs can be built with little trouble, it is usually cheaper to use one of the many DAC i.c.p.s available. These have the resistor network, FET switches, etc. in one easily-used package.

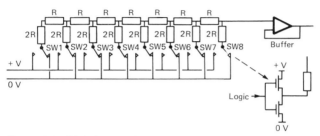

Figure 5.11. Digital to analog converter

It is desirable to isolate analog outputs, but in practice this is not as easy to achieve as for digital outputs. LEDs and phototransistors are very non-linear devices, making isolation somewhat complex. Isolation amplifiers use either pulse width modulation or amplitude modulation techniques on an AC carrier which is then passed through an opto-isolator or transformer. On the plant side the signal is demodulated again. Isolation amplifiers can be purchased at reasonable prices, but will be a significant part of the cost of an industrial interface.

Analog inputs
Before an analog signal can be read by a microprocessor, the signal must first be converted to a digital binary signal. This is done by a circuit called an Analog to Digital Converter (or ADC). There are four common ways of achieving the conversion, each with its own particular advantages.

The Flash, or parallel, converter of *Fig. 5.12* is used where a high-speed, low-accuracy ADC is required. The incoming voltage is compared with an array of reference voltages, and the comparator outputs decoded to give a binary signal. Conversion times of better than 1 µS are possible, but the circuit complexity increases rapidly for increased resolution. Eight comparators are needed for three bits, four bits need 16 comparators and so on.

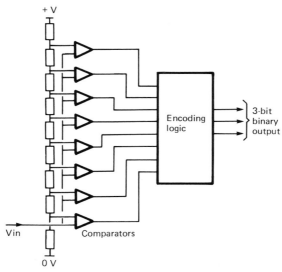

Figure 5.12. Flash analog to digital converter

The Ramp converter, shown in *Fig. 5.13*, is a reasonable compromise between speed, complexity and expense. A typical circuit will give a resolution of one part in 255 and a conversion time of about 1 ms. The operation starts with a 'convert' command which sets the memory FFI and resets the counter. FFI gates clock pulses to the counter, which counts up. The counter output is connected to a DAC whose output is compared with the input voltage. When the DAC output equals the input voltage, the comparator resets FFI, stopping

142

the counter and giving a ready signal to indicate that conversion is complete. The counter now holds a binary representation of the input voltage. A variation of the Ramp ADC, known as a Tracking ADC, uses an up/down counter which is not reset at the start of each conversion.

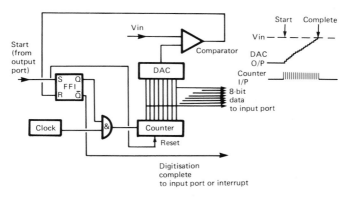

Figure 5.13. Ramp analog to digital converter

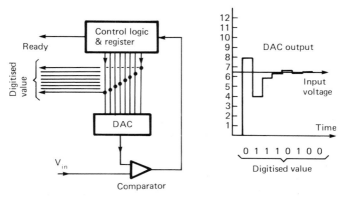

Figure 5.14. Successive approximation ADC

143

The Successive Approximation converter is a high-speed, high-accuracy ADC. Although not as fast as the flash ADC, conversion times of about 10 µS and an accuracy of one part in 1000 are more than adequate for most applications. A successive approximation circuit, shown on *Fig. 5.14*, tests one bit at a time from most significant to least significant bit. The conversion thus takes the same number of clock pulses as there are bits in the output (unlike the ramp ADC which uses the same number of clock pulses as the counter content). The control logic is slightly more complex than that for the ramp ADC, which increases the cost.

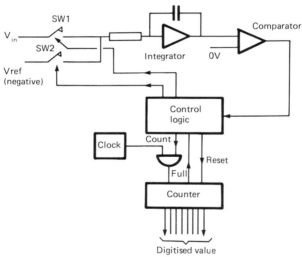

Figure 5.15. Dual ramp ADC

The final type of ADC, illustrated in *Fig. 5.15*, is known as an Integrator ADC (the term Dual Ramp is sometimes used). At the start of the conversion, switch SW1 is closed and the input voltage is integrated. As the integrator output crosses 0 V, the counter is started. Integration continues until the counter reaches full count. The counter is reset, SW1 opens and SW2 closes. Since Vr is negative, the integrator output

144

starts to fall. The counter is started again, and runs until the integrator output reaches 0 V again. The counter now holds a digital representation of Vin. The integrator ADC is the slowest of the ADCs described, but is probably the most accurate. The accuracy does not depend on the component values or clock frequency and offset errors cancel out.

Whatever analog inputs are required, one of the four ADC types will be suitable (although the price might come as a nasty surprise). It will probably come as no surprise to learn that ready-made ADCs in i.c.p. and encapsulated form are cheaper than home-made units.

Multiplexers Unless exceptionally high speeds are required, usually one ADC will suffice for all analog inputs. A multiplexer is similar to a rotary switch, selecting analog

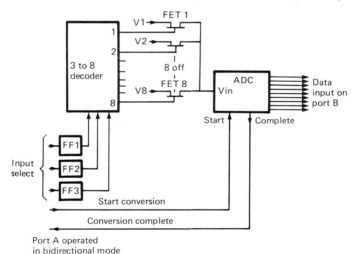

Figure 5.16. Analog multiplexer and ADC

inputs one at a time for conversion by the ADC. In the circuit of *Fig. 5.16*, inputs are selected by FETs 1 to 8, which are in turn controlled by the three flip-flops FF1 to FF3. To make a measurement, the computer sends a three-bit input-select word and a start command to port A. When the conversion is complete port A interrupts the computer, which can then read the value from port B.

Sample and hold circuits Problems can be caused if the inputs are varying rapidly. A sample and hold circuit takes a 'snapshot picture' of the input, which is then used by the ADC. The sample and hold circuit of *Fig. 5.17* freezes the input voltage on a capacitor. Usually one sample and hold circuit will be used between the multiplexer and the ADC.

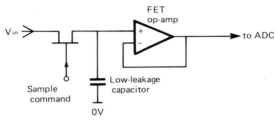

Figure 5.17. Sample and hold circuit

Analog scanners A typical analog input unit will incorporate sixteen isolation amplifiers and gain-setting stages, a sixteen-way multiplexer, sample and hold, twelve-bit ADC, and interface logic. The whole unit is known as an analog scanner.

Where sensors such as thermocouples or flow transducers are being monitored, the raw signals will be converted to standard signals by signal-conditioning cards at the sensors. A common standard on analog inputs uses 4–20 mA to represent zero to full-scale. The use of a current to transmit the value gives noise rejection, and the offset zero gives indication of a sensor failure or a cable fault.

Programming for control

The prime requirement for control programs is speed. In general, in commercial computing the time taken to run a program is not a major consideration. In control computing the outside world will not wait for the computer to decide what to do next, and programs must be designed for maximum speed.

Interpreters such as BASIC are very slow, and have a rather restrictive instruction set. All control applications beyond simple data loggers run in machine-code programs originally written in assembly languages or for compilers. The UK language CORAL is particularly well suited for control applications.

The high speed of microcomputers allow them to be used as part of feedback loops. Early computer control schemes used techniques similar to *Fig. 5.18*. The computer calculated the desired value of the controlled variable, and output an

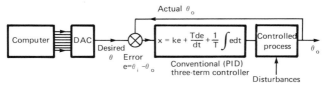

Figure 5.18. Supervisory computer control

analog set point. Conventional electronic controllers performed the error calculation and three-term control. This is known as Supervisory Control.

A typical modern scheme would use the computer to close the feedback loop as shown in *Fig. 5.19*. The controlled variable is measured directly by the computer, and the error calculation and three-term control performed by program. Apart from reducing the hardware costs, this approach does not suffer from the drift problems associated with conventional controllers. This technique is called Direct Digital Control (DDC).

Computer control has many attractions for the control engineer. In a conventional system, design, construction, installation and commissioning are sequential operations. In a computer system, the hardware is simply an adequate amount of digital and analog I/O which can be ordered at an early stage in the project. Design (i.e. writing the program) and construction/installation become parallel operations with considerable time and cost savings.

The biggest advantage, however, comes at the commissioning stage. Very few jobs go in as planned, and design changes

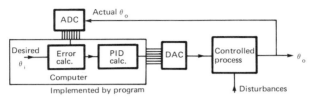

Figure 5.19. Direct digital control

can be difficult, lengthy and expensive at a late stage. In a computer system, most changes will be implemented by program modifications without significant delay.

Safety

No electronic equipment can be totally fail-safe, which presents several problems for the control engineer. Obviously, different standards would be applied to a microcomputer being used to control a domestic washing machine, and a microcomputer controlling the gas/air ratio in a furnace, but regardless of the system the designer should consider what could occur after a failure.

The first line of defence against a computer failure is usually a Watchdog Timer, or WDT. This is an output device to which the computer sends a test output at regular intervals (typically 50 Hz). If the rate changes (due to the computer going into a loop for example) or the test data is incorrect, the WDT forces all outputs to a predetermined, safe state.

Critical outputs will require three or more independent signals to be present before an action will occur. In extreme cases a majority vote system will be used, with differences initiating alarms. Essential inputs will be at least duplicated.

Although absolute safety cannot be guaranteed, the probability of catastrophic failure can be predicted with a knowledge of component failure rates. With the techniques outlined above, the probability can be made acceptably small. Needless to say, the cost of the system rises accordingly!

6

Microprocessor families

There are many eight-bit microprocessors, but four families have emerged as industry standards: the 6502, 8080, 6800 and Z-80. Between them they account for 95 per cent of the domestic and business microcomputer market, and around 75 per cent of the whole field of microcomputers. This chapter describes these devices and their support chips, plus brief descriptions of other less common microprocessors. It is not the intention to give a 'best buy' as different microprocessors have different advantages and disadvantages.

The MOS technology 6502

The 6502 is one of the more successful microprocessors, being used on the popular Apple, PET, BBC, Electron and Acorn range of microcomputers. It is one of the simpler microprocessors, and probably one of the easiest to program in machine code. To a programmer it can be represented by *Fig. 6.1*.

Compared with the hypothetical microprocessor described in Chapter 2, *Fig. 6.1* is very simple. The 6502 has a single register/accumulator, two index registers, a flag register (called the processor status word or PSW), an eight-bit stack pointer (SP) to which we will return later, and the 16-bit program counter. This simplicity is both the strength, and weakness, of the 6502. Although there are few instructions, the single register makes programming rather tedious.

The instruction set for the 6502 contains 152 operable instructions. There is no perfect instruction set, and in the 6502 set there are several useful instructions, and several omissions. One of the most frustrating of these is the lack of a single-word increment and decrement instruction operating directly on the accumulator. Where increment and decrement are required, ADD immediate 01, or SUB immediate 01, have to be used, which are two-word instructions.

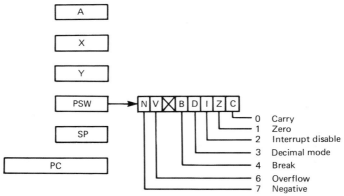

Figure 6.1. The 6502

The 6502 has one of the most versatile set of indexed instructions. There are two eight-bit index registers, X and Y. An indexed instruction has the form Function Base Address which occupies three words (e.g. BD 50 0C is load A indexed X, base address 0C50). The processor adds the contents of the index register to the base address to give the actual address. If, in the above example, X contained 17, we would load A with the contents of location 0C67.

There is no real indirect addressing on the 6502, but the X register can be used to indicate two successive locations in page zero which contain the target address. These are two-word instructions, the second byte containing a number which is added to the contents of X to give the first address in page zero.

Indirect addressing with the Y register is slightly different. A two-word instruction directly identifies a page zero address which, with the succeeding location, gives a 16-bit base address. The contents of Y are added to the base address to give the target address. The X register form is called Indexed Indirect, and the Y register form, somewhat confusingly, Indirect Indexed.

A subroutine call (Jump Subroutine, JSR) is only available in unconditional direct form (a three-byte instruction, e.g. 20 00 10, JSR 1000). Conditional jumps to subroutines must be handled by conditional jumps (known as branches) before the actual JSR instruction. The single-byte return (RTS) instruction is only available in unconditional form.

Discussion of subroutines brings us naturally to the stack pointer. The stack can only be placed on page one (addresses 0100 to 01FF in hex). The stack pointer holds the low byte, so if SP holds D5 the actual stack address is 01D5. Normally the stack will start at 01FF and work down. Rather annoyingly, the stack pointer register can only be loaded by a transfer from X.

The stack can also be used to save other data, but only the accumulator and the PSW can be pushed directly on to the stack (and retrieved later of course). The index registers, X and Y, cannot be saved directly. To save all registers, it is necessary to Push A, Push PSW, Transfer X to A, Push A, Transfer Y to A, Push A. Retrieving the data is done by Pull operations and transfers back to Y and X. The sequence is not difficult, but uses more instructions than other microprocessors.

Memory mapped I/O is used by the 6502, which means all I/O devices are treated as store locations (see Chapters 4 and 5). Communication to a serial link is performed with conventional UARTs in a manner identical to that described in Chapter 4. Parallel outputs are usually achieved with the 6520 PIO chip shown diagramatically in *Fig. 6.2*.

The 6520 generally follows the principles outlined in Chapter 5, having two ports (denoted A and B) which can be used as inputs, outputs or combined input/output bits. Each port has a control register, CR, and a data direction register, DDR, which defines which bits are inputs and which are outputs.

Register selection is achieved by A0 and A1 which are normally the least significant bits of the address highway. External address decode logic is connected to the chip select pin.

Interrupt handling is not the 6502's strong point, and is distinctly rudimentary compared to, say, the Z-80. The 6502 can deal with two forms of interrupts, maskable and non-maskable. A maskable interrupt can be ignored by program,

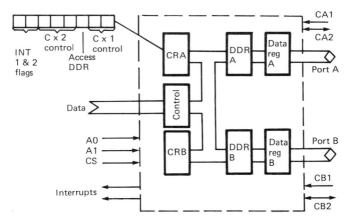

Figure 6.2. The 6502 PIO device

a non-maskable interrupt cannot. Control instructions (Enable Interrupts, Disable Interrupts) are used to allow, and block, maskable interrupts.

When an interrupt occurs the 6502 completes the current instruction and pushes the program counter and the PSW on to the stack. Register A, X and Y are not saved automatically. They must be saved by the programmer at the start of the interrupt service routine and restored on leaving the service routine. The interrupt is acknowledged, and the 6502 jumps to the instruction at location FFFE (for maskable interrupts) or FFFA (for non-maskable interrupts). These locations contain branch instructions to the actual service routines.

The 6502 must then poll the peripherals to see which device generated the interrupt. There is no facility for the interrupting device to identify itself.

The arrangement of the interrupt handling on the 6502 is not particularly elegant. The hardware must contain RAM (or ROM) at locations FFFA to FFFF, and the programmer is

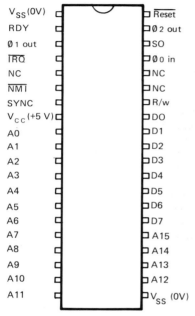

Figure 6.3. Pinning for 6502

forced to waste instructions (and time) polling the peripherals. For these reasons the 6502 is not widely used in control computing and is best suited to business machines.

The 6502 pin arrangement is shown in *Fig. 6.3*. A single phase 1 MHz clock is used, which generates internally φ1 and φ2 for bus timing.

The Motorola 6800

The 6800 is not used in any common business or home computer, but is quite popular with industrial users and the DIY amateur. Although it does not have the comprehensive instruction set of the 8085 or the Z-80, the 6800's appeal lies in having a very useful family of support devices.

The 6800 can be represented by the block diagram of *Fig. 6.4.* There is an obvious family resemblance to the 6502 described above, although the 6502 and 6800 were designed separately by two different manufacturers.

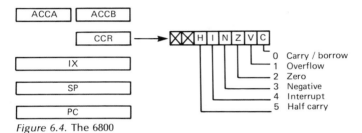

Figure 6.4. The 6800

Two eight-bit accumulators are provided (Acc A and Acc B), both of which can be used for arithmetic. A and B are true accumulators, unlike most other multi-register micro-processors, which use one register as an accumulator and the rest as one-byte temporary storage. Flags are held in the Condition Code Register CCR as shown.

The advantage of the two accumulators is marred by the 6800's major drawback; the single IX index register. Given the choice of two accumulators and two index registers, most programmers would prefer the extra index register, but it is largely a matter of personal preference.

The 6800 uses six addressing modes. Immediate, extended and inherent addressing operate exactly as described in Chapter 3. Indexed addressing uses the 16-bit index register as the base address and the instruction contains the offset. Page-zero addressing is available on most instructions, but is somewhat confusingly called Direct Addressing, a term used by other manufacturers for extended addressing.

Jumps and subroutine calls can use relative, indexed or extended addressing. Conditional jumps only use relative addressing. There are no conditional jumps to subroutines or conditional return from subroutine instructions.

The stack pointer is held in the 16-bit SP register, allowing the stack to be placed at any convenient point in the RAM. The stack pointer can be loaded from memory with immediate, extended or page-zero instructions. It cannot be loaded from the accumulator.

The 6800 handles interrupts in a very elementary manner. Interrupts are daisy-chained to provide an Interrupt Request signal. This is not acknowledged by the processor. On receipt of the request, the processor saves ALL registers and accumulators on the stack (very good feature) and jumps to location FFF8 (maskable interrupt), or FFFC (non-maskable interrupt). These locations will contain a jump to the actual service routine.

The 6800 does not handle vectored interrupts, so the service routine must first poll the peripherals to find the device initiating the request. The 6800 family, however, contains the 6828 priority interrupt controller which can be used to generate vectored interrupts by stealing control of the address bus when FFF8 or FFFC appears.

The interrupt service routine ends with a Return from Interrupt instruction which pulls the accumulators and registers from the stack.

A useful set of I/O chips is provided in the 6800 family. All I/O is memory mapped, and there is no real facility for separate I/O addressing. The parallel I/O chip 6820 is called a Peripheral Interface Adaptor (PIA) and is shown in *Fig. 6.5*. The PIA comprises two ports whose operating modes are selected by the control registers.

The data direction registers determine which bits are inputs, and which are outputs. Handshake signals are provided for each port.

Pin connections for the 6800 are shown in *Fig. 6.6*. The device operates on a single 5 volt supply and requires an external two-phase 1 MHz clock.

The 6800 was one of the earlier microprocessors, and does

show its age in comparison with the 8080 and Z-80 described below. An updated 6800, called the 6809 has been released which overcomes many of the limitations of the 6800. The 6809 is used in the popular Dragon computer.

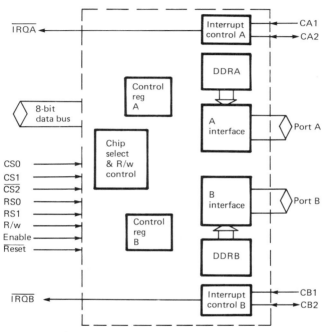

Figure 6.5. The 6820 peripheral interface adaptor

The programmer's view of the 6809 is shown in *Fig. 6.7.* Two accumulators A and B are still provided, but these can now be used as two eight-bit accumulators or one 16-bit accumulator. A second index register (IY) has been added, which removes the major weakness of the 6800. A new register, Direct Page, or DP, is used with the direct address mode to provide the high byte of the address. In the 6800 direct mode was limited to page zero. Two stack pointers, U

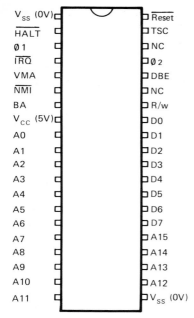

Figure 6.6. 6800 pinning

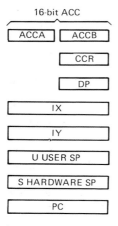

Figure 6.7. The 6809

158

and S, are provided (a unique feature) which allows the programmer to keep two separate stacks.

The 6809 will run 6800 programs, but several useful instructions have been added. Indirect addressing is allowed, and more indexed addressing modes. A particularly notable instruction is the eight-bit multiply which is unique to the 6809.

There have also been hardware improvements. Interrupt acknowledge and other improved interrupt handling is included, and an on-chip clock obviates the need for an external oscillator.

The 6800 and 6809 are part of a well-thought-out family of support devices including UARTs, PIAs, ROMs, RAMs and bus extenders. This compatible range of chips allows a system designer to 'bolt together' a system with little design effort. This instant computer approach is the real charm of the 6800, and makes it a popular choice for the small-system, and amateur, constructor.

The Intel 8080

The 8080 is one of the more powerful microprocessors, but is more likely to be encountered in industrial-control microcomputers than in home or business machines. The programmer's block diagram, in *Fig. 6.8*, is obviously more complex than the 6502 or the 6800 which means that programming is more complex, but usually more efficient.

The first obvious difference from the previous microprocessors is the register set, all eight of them. Register A is the accumulator, and is the only register that can be used as the destination for arithmetical and logical operations. The PSW (processor status word) is the flag register. Registers B, C, D, E, H and L are six general-purpose registers used for temporary storage.

These registers speed up the operation of a program considerably, because all inter-register operations are single-byte instructions (and hence only access the store once).

The registers also have another advantage, which is just as important. These six registers can be treated as three 16-bit

registers BC, DE, HL. These three register pairs can hold the
address for register indirect instructions, and can be used in
a limited number of 16-bit arithmetic instructions.

The instruction set has the usual notable omissions and
additions. There is no indexed addressing on the 8080, but
this is not the disadvantage it might appear. The register

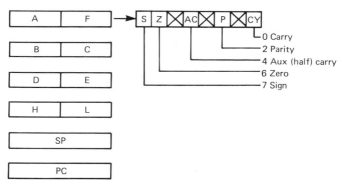

Figure 6.8. The 8080

indirect mode really fulfills the same purpose because indexed addressing is usually used to process lists, and the 16-bit
register pairs can be incremented and decremented directly.
Another obvious omission is relative addressing. The 8080
simply uses direct addressing for all jumps and subroutine
calls.

The big advantage of the 8080 instruction set is the vast
array of inter-register operations. Eight-bit and 16-bit data can
be shunted between registers and used in arithmetic operations with single-byte instructions. A unique feature is an
immediate register indirect write to memory, with HL holding
the address. Sixteen-bit data can also be moved between
register pair HL and two adjacent store locations with one
three-byte (extended address) instruction.

The 8080 uses a 16-bit stack pointer, allowing the stack to
be placed at any convenient point in the store. All register

pairs can be pushed on to the stack (or pulled off the stack) with a one-byte instruction. The accumulator and PSW are treated as a register pair for push and pop instructions.

All jump and subroutine calls use extended addressing. A very useful set of conditional subroutine calls and conditional return instructions is provided in addition to the usual conditional jump instruction.

Input/output on the 8080 can be managed as memory mapped I/O, but IN and OUT instructions are also provided

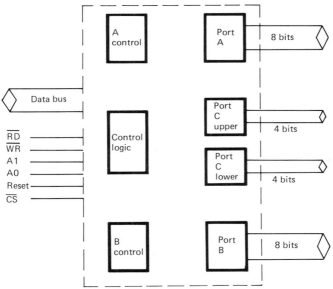

Figure 6.9. The 8255 programmable peripheral interface

for individually addressed ports. To use these instructions the 8228 system control i.c.p. needs to be added to give separate memory and I/O control signals.

Parallel I/O is performed via the 8255 Programmable Peripheral Interface (PPI, yet another set of letters for a PIO chip!) shown in *Fig. 6.9*. This has 24 I/O connections which can be operated in three modes as selected by the control register. In mode 0, the I/O connections can be selected as inputs or outputs in blocks of four with no handshaking. In mode 1, ports A and B can be selected to be inputs or outputs, and the C port connections are used for handshakes and interrupts. The final mode 2 is a bidirectional mode.

Interrupt handling is one of the 8080's strong points. Although polled interrupts can be used, the 8080 usually employs a peripheral-generated vector to identify the servicing routine required. When an interrupt occurs, the 8080 finishes its current instruction, then sends an interrupt acknowledge.

The interrupting peripheral now forces an *instruction* on to the data bus. Conveniently the 8080 has eight RST instructions which are single-byte subroutine calls to hex addresses 0, 8, 10, 18, 20, 28, 30, 38.

The peripheral forces an RST instruction, which causes the processor to obey a subroutine call to one of the eight hex addresses above. Because the processor is, effectively, obeying a subroutine call, only the program counter is pushed on to the stack. The flag and other registers must be saved by the programmer. Normally the instruction at the RST address will be a jump to the servicing routine.

Up to eight service routines (and eight interrupting peripherals) can be handled without polling. More peripherals can of course be handled easily by arranging them into eight groups which use the eight RST instructions, so 24 interrupting devices would only require three devices to be polled in each service routine.

The 8080 pin connections are shown in *Fig. 6.10*, which shows the 8080's major disadvantage. Three supplies are needed ($+12$ V, $+5$ V and -5 V). This is not quite the problem it would seem as several of the popular RAM i.c.p.s also require these voltages. A two-phase clock is needed, which is usually provided by the 8224 clock generator i.c.p.

The 8080 became very popular for industrial control, but it has been replaced to some extent by the Intel 8085 (known to its users as the 8080GT). The 8085 is an improved 8080, and all 8080 programs will run on an 8085. It does have some added advantages however.

The 8085 only requires a single 5 volt supply, and has an internal 3 MHz clock generator. On the 8080 a bus driver i.c.p. (8228) is required to interface with PIO devices. The 8085 interfaces with PIO devices directly.

One more interesting feature is the multiplexed data address bus. The address and data are not required on the

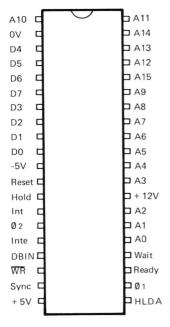

Figure 6.10. Pinning for the 8080

highway at the same time, so bits 0 to 7 on the address bus are also used for data. Signals on the control bus identify whether an address or data is present.

A simple eight-bit latch can be used to provide a normal 16-bit address bus and eight-bit data bus as shown on *Fig. 6.11*, but the 8085 is normally used with Intel's own RAM which contains a demultiplexer and can connect directly to the 8085 bus.

163

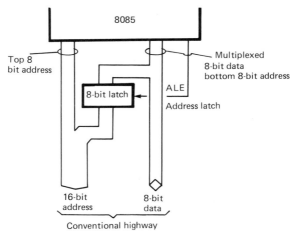

Figure 6.11. Demultiplexing the 8085 highways

The 8085 has a large family of support chips, timers, PIO, RAM, DMA controllers, bus arbitration and the AMD arithmetic chip, to name but a few. It is widely used for industrial control, and is the basis of the GEM-80 system described in Chapter 7.

The Zilog Z-80

The astute reader may have noticed a slight pro-Z-80 bias. Some of this bias arises from the simple fact that the author's own Nascom is Z-80 based, but the Z-80 was chosen for illustration purposes in this book because it is the most powerful eight-bit microprocessor available.

The Z-80 has become a very popular microprocessor, being used in the TRS-80, Nascom, Video Genie, Sharp MKS-80 and Sinclair ZX81 and Spectrum, among others. Its powerful I/O features (described below) make it ideally suited for industrial control, and it is the basis of many process control schemes.

The Z-80 is based on the 8080, and all 8080 programs will run on a Z-80 without modification. The designers added many improvements and additional instructions. These start with the programmer's model of *Fig. 6.12*. The Z-80 has two register sets, called main and alternate. The processor can work on either set and switch with a one-byte exchange instruction. Data in the register set not in use is not lost, and

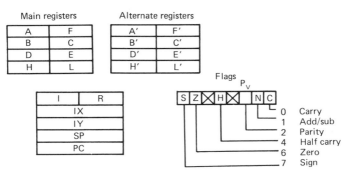

Figure 6.12. The Z-80

can be used later with another exchange instruction. The programmer thus has two accumulators (each with its own flag register) and 12 general-purpose registers (which can also be used as six 16-bit register pairs).

Lack of indexed addressing was one of the 8080's faults; the Z-80 has two index registers IX and IY. These are 16-bit index registers, and are used to supply the base address with the instruction providing the offset. The register set on the Z-80 is so comprehensive that it is actually possible to build a Z-80 based microcomputer with just ROM memory, all temporary storage being provided by the registers.

The R register is another of the Z-80's useful features. Most microcomputers use dynamic RAM which requires refreshing every few milliseconds. Normally this refreshing is done by logic local to the RAM. The R register in a Z-80 is a memory refresh counter, whose contents are forced on to the lower portion of the address bus along with a refresh signal on the control bus. The R register is incremented after each instruction, refreshing every store location in a millisecond or so. The operation of this refreshing is totally transparent to the user.

The I register (interrupt vector) is used with interrupts and will be described later along with the Z-80's powerful I/O facilities.

The Z-80 has the most comprehensive instruction set of any eight-bit microprocessor. All the addressing modes and instruction types described in Chapter 3 are used, and many 16-bit arithmetic functions can be performed.

Jump instructions can be performed in extended, relative and register indirect modes. Conditional jumps use extended and relative modes. Conditional calls to subroutines and conditional returns are provided. A particularly useful instruction for constructing loops is 'Decrement B, jump relative if B non-zero'. Register B is loaded with the loop counter before the sequence starts as below:

```
Load B   Immediate count
Loop sequence
Dec B Jump non-zero
```

The loop sequence will be performed 'count' times.

The Z-80 uses a 16-bit stack pointer, so the stack can be located at any convenient point in RAM. The stack pointer can be loaded in immediate mode from HL or (using extended addressing) direct from a store location.

Block transfers are a powerful set of instructions unique to the Z-80. These allow blocks of data to be moved around the store. Top down or bottom up transfers can be performed, so overlapping addresses can be used. Register pair HL holds the source location, DE the destination, and BC the number of bytes to be transferred. A closely related (and equally useful) instruction set is the 'block search'. These allow a block of memory to be searched for a particular bit pattern.

The Z-80 has an extensive set of I/O instructions. Memory mapped I/O can be used, but usually separate I/O address and the Z-80 special I/O instructions are used. Immediate or register indirect addressing is used, and a powerful block transfer set of I/O instructions are provided which move data in both directions between I/O ports and a block of memory. These block transfer functions are particularly useful when driving printers.

One of the attractions of the Z-80 is its versatility in dealing with interrupts. There are three ways in which interrupts can be handled. The first is identical to the 8080 outlined above, and is included to make the Z-80 totally program-compatible with the 8080. The second simply calls location hex 0038, and is similar in principle to the procedure used by the 6502 or 6800.

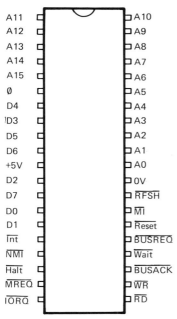

Figure 6.13. Pinning for the Z-80

The final mode is unique to the Z-80 and is probably the most versatile. When an interrupt occurs, and is acknowledged, the peripheral forces a byte on to the data bus. The processor uses this data along with the contents of the I register to form a 16-bit address (high byte from the I register, low byte from the peripheral) which is the start of the servicing routine. The contents of the I register can be changed at any time by the program. The low byte from the peripheral is held in the PIO and is loaded by an output command to the PIO interrupt vector register.

When the CPU services an interrupt, only the program counter is automatically saved on the stack. The programmer must arrange to save the other registers.

The Z-80 pin connections are shown in *Fig. 6.13*. A single-phase clock of 1, 2 or 4 MHz (dependent on version) and a single 5 volt supply are required.

The Z-80 has a useful family of support chips, including UARTs, PIOs, and timer chips. All the 8080 support chips can be used with the Z-80 with little difficulty. If the interrupt vector facility is required, however, this can only be found on the Z-80's own devices.

The Z-80 belongs to a different generation of micros from the 6502/6800, and has correspondingly more facilities and a richer instruction set. It is, however, correspondingly more difficult to program until the user has gained some experience. It is probably the most popular micro with professional programmers.

Less common devices

The 6502, 6800, 8080 and Z-80 between them probably cover about 75 per cent of the microcomputer world, although every semiconductor manufacturer has produced his own microprocessor. In the rest of this chapter a few less common microprocessors are briefly described.

Mullard/Signetics 2650
This device should not be confused with the 6502. In the author's opinion the 2650 is a rather neglected device as it does have its own peculiar charm. The programmer's model is shown in *Fig. 6.14*. It has seven accumulators which can all be used for arithmetic purposes (an advantage over even the all-powerful Z-80).

168

An interesting feature is the on-chip stack. Up to eight addresses can be held on the stack. This does mean that subroutines can only be nested eight deep, but was included to allow systems to be built with only ROM memory.

The charm of the 2650 lies in the logical way in which its instruction set has been made up. (It is, in fact, almost a binary version of Marvin from Chapter 1.) An instruction

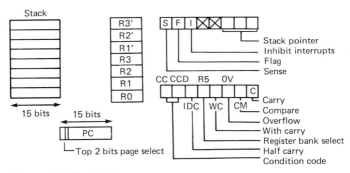

Figure 6.14. The 2650

consists of a logical instruction code, a register number, and one or two additional bytes depending on which of the six addressing modes (register, immediate, relative, absolute, absolute branch or indirect) is being used.

The 2650 can only address 32K of store which could be a problem in larger systems. Despite this, its well-thought-out instruction set makes it an ideal microprocessor for the newcomer, and it really deserves more coverage than it has received to date.

National Semiconductor SC/MP

The SC/MP was one of the earlier microprocessors, and is showing signs of its age. It is very popular, though, with DIY computer enthusiasts working in machine code. The programmer's model is shown in *Fig. 6.15*. Four 16-bit registers are accessible, R0 is the PC, R3 holds the address of the

169

interrupt service routine, and R1, R2 can be used as general-purpose address pointers. In addition there is an eight-bit accumulator and an eight-bit extension register.

The address modes available on the SC/MP are rather limited. Most memory addressing is done in a mixture of relative and indexed addressing by specifying an R register

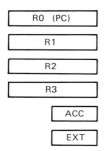

RO (PC)

R1

R2

R3

ACC

EXT

Figure 6.15. The SC/MP

and an offset. If R0 is specified we have relative addressing, if R1 or R2 is specified we have indexed addressing. There is no absolute addressing, so instructions are only one or two bytes in length. Immediate addressing is provided.

The SC/MP has a 12-bit address highway, although a multiplexed scheme is used on the top four bits to allow 64K to be addressed with external latches. An on-chip oscillator is provided. The chip can run with CMOS on a single 12 volt supply, or with TTL on a split $+5V -7V$ supply.

In conclusion, the SC/MP is not likely to be considered by any designer of a new system. It is slow and has a rather clumsy architecture and instruction set. A SC/MP-based small system is quite easy to build, however, and many useful amateur designs have been published.

Intersil IM6100

The PDP8 was the first successful minicomputer introduced in the 1960s, and consequently has a vast array of off-the-shelf software available. The IM6100 is designed to simulate the CPU of a PDP8-E. In common with the PDP8, the IM6100 is a 12-bit machine, utilising a 12-bit data word and a 12-bit address. All the instructions of the PDP8 are recognised.

The chip features an on-chip crystal clock, and a single 12-bit multiplexed address/data bus. Intersil's own ROMs and RAMs incorporate demultiplexer logic and latches so no external logic is required to separate the address and data. The device runs on a 5 volt supply.

The IM6100 is invaluable to anyone who has a cupboard full of PDP8 programs, but is not really suitable for other applications. The PDP8 itself is rather an archaic machine, and the IM6100 compares poorly with more modern microprocessors.

7

Applications of micro-computers

The microcomputer is a versatile device, and is to be found in many varied applications. In this chapter several interesting uses of the microcomputer are described. The topics chosen are, of course, only a small selection of many.

Toys and games

Mankind has always been fascinated by toys, and it is not surprising that there are many microprocessor-based toys on the market. Although derided by some professional computer experts, they do employ some very ingenious circuitry. Of particular interest is the fact that many employ a true computer on a chip.

Semiconductor manufacturers have recognised the need for a small dedicated microcomputer, and have produced microcomputer i.c.p.s for large volume purchasers. These i.c.p.s contain the CPU, I/O, a small amount of RAM and the user's pre-programmed ROM in the one device. The only connections to the outside world are therefore the I/O connections and power supplies.

A typical microcomputer on a chip is the Texas Instruments TMS 1000 shown in block diagram in *Fig. 7.1*. The device stores its programs in a 1K by 1 byte ROM, arranged as 16 pages of 64 words per page. The ROM is thus addressed by a six-bit program counter and four-bit page address register. The RAM is organised as 64 words of four bits per word addressed as 16 pages of four words per page. The Y register selects the page, and the X register the word within the page.

Arithmetic is performed by a four-bit accumulator and ALU. Apart from the short word length, this is fairly conventional and provides all the usual arithmetic functions and flags.

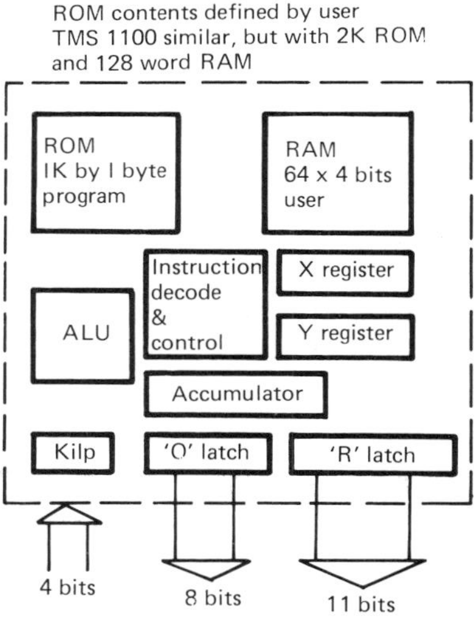

Figure 7.1. TMS 1000. 'Computer on a Chip'

Communication to the outside world is performed by 19 output lines and four input lines. This does not mean, however, that the device is restricted to four inputs. The R outputs are designed to be used as address outputs to provide multiplexed inputs, using techniques similar to those described for electronic keyboards in Chapter 4. *Fig. 7.2* shows 16 inputs being scanned by four R outputs. The R outputs can also be used to address external latches to extend the number of outputs that can be driven.

The TMS 1000 has 43 basic instructions covering I/O, data transfer, arithmetic, conditional jumps and even subroutines. It is possible for the user to define his own instructions to some extent because a mask-programmable logic array is included as part of the instruction decoder.

The Big Trak of *Fig. 7.3* uses the TMS 1000. This very ingenious toy is a programmable tank whose actions are loaded via its calculator-type keyboard. The tank can obey a 16-step program incorporating forward and reverse motions

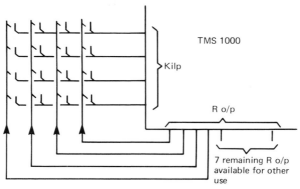

Figure 7.2. Scanning inputs on the TMS 1000

Figure 7.3. The computer-controlled 'Big Trak'

of programmable distances, turns left or right through programmable angles, pauses for programmable times and the firing of its 'laser gun'. These actions are all accompanied by well-chosen sound effects.

Internally Big Trak can be represented by *Fig. 7.4*. The tank is driven by two independently-controlled motors, driven off four 0 outputs. The distance travelled, and the angle turned, are measured by a pulse generator connected to input K8 and strobed by R7. The keyboard is strobed by R0 to R6 and read

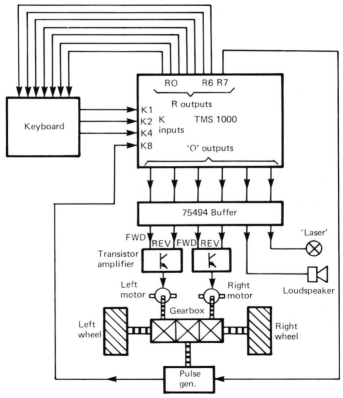

Figure 7.4. Schematic of 'Big Trak'

on K1, K2 and K4. The sound effects speaker and laser gun light are driven by 0 outputs. The internal electronics of Big Trak thus consists of four transistors, an eight-bit buffer/driver, a few resistors and capacitors and a TMS 1000 computer. Despite the simplicity of its circuit, the ingenuity of the programmers makes it a most entertaining toy.

Big Trak itself is a useful introduction to the concept of programming, and its 'language' resembles the educational language LOGO. Big Traks are being used by some primary schools for teaching purposes.

The techniques used in Big Trak are similar to those in most computer toys. It should be noted, though, that many toy manufactureres bend the truth a little and describe all toys using i.c.p.s as 'computer-controlled'. Most of the simpler TV games use i.c.p. technology, but are not true computers.

Many programmable TV games are, however, real computers, with games-orientated VDUs. Character generator ROMs are readily available to give racing cars, cowboys, ships, invading aliens, and all the other symbols needed. Arcade game manufacturers have long recognised that the public rapidly tire of a particular game. Most arcade machines can be withdrawn, re-programmed with a new game, and placed back in service at relatively little cost when public tastes change.

It used to be said (not so long ago) that a computer could never play a good game of chess. The microcomputer has surprised many people by playing chess at a level that would easily beat an average player and give most club players a hard game.

Chess-playing computers are available at a wide range of prices, the depth of the analysis and speed of response determining the price. It is a sobering experience to be beaten by one of these machines. The hardware of these machines is usually simple; a microprocessor, about 16K of program in ROM and the I/O interface for the keyboard and display. The clever part is obviously the program and, again obviously, this book is too short to discuss the subtleties of techniques such as search trees and the alpha-beta algorithm. A chess-playing program (Sargon) available for home

176

microcomputers is recommended for readers interested in this field.

A quick glance through computing magazines will show that a large percentage of the programs sold for home computers are games in one form or another. Although again derided by professionals, some of these games are great fun and very addictive. Particularly well-suited to the home computer are the Adventure type games (based on the fantasy game Dungeons and Dragons) where the player explores an underground cave system and battles with dragons, trolls and giants to discover fabulous treasure.

The computer is also well suited to acting as referee and opponent in wargames. These inherently complex games convert well to computer programs, and gain considerably in realism as the computer can blur the information available to the players. At least one wargame manufacturer (Avalon Hill) is selling wargame programs on discs for TRS-80 and Apple computers.

Robots

For some reason, robots and microprocessors have become linked in most people's minds. The reality, like most microprocessor myths, is somewhat disappointing. At the time of writing there are very few robots in operation; current estimates are about 10 000 robots world-wide, and about 400 in the UK. Compared to a UK working population of about 25 million, the impact of robots to date can only be described as negligible.

Despite this gloomy picture, it is widely thought by industrial engineers that there will be a sudden boom in robot applications in the very near future, as labour costs will undoubtedly continue to rise and robot costs fall. All robots require a computer as the central controller, and the microprocessor is well suited to this task.

Robots are the natural development of the numerically-controlled machine tool. Digital, and computer, controlled lathes, millers, grinders and drilling machines have been very common for many years, and have reached a high degree of sophistication. A robot, however, is a general-purpose machine, and unlike an NC machine tool it is not limited to one task.

An industrial robot bears little, if any, resemblance to the humanoid robots beloved of science fiction writers and film producers. Most robots are constructed in a manner similar to *Fig. 7.5a* or b and consist of an articulated arm mechanism and an operational head. In general, there are four classes of robots.

The transfer (or pick and place) robot is used to move an item from one place to another. A common application is the transfer of a blank metal plate from a conveyor belt to a press, followed by the transfer of the finished pressing to a box. The operational head is obviously some form of gripper device.

Paint-spraying robots are used in the motor car and domestic appliance industries. The operational head is a paint spray fed with paint and compressed air down flexible tubing. The motion required from the head will be very complex to ensure even coverage in all the nooks and crannies of the sprayed object. Paint-spraying robots are therefore more complex than transfer robots.

Welding robots are becoming quite common in the motor car industry. Welding can be done either by spot welds or continuous welds. The former is used mostly for car bodies, the latter for pressure vessels and pipes. A spot welder requires a gripper-type head, a continuous welder a feed-mechanism head for the wire and flux.

The final robot type is the assembler, used to construct an item from its component parts. At present there are no real units in operation, as rudimentary vision and tactile sensors are needed which are prohibitively expensive and rather unreliable. Several assembly robots have been built in university research departments, and it is probable that these will develop into commercial units in the near future.

Whatever the application, the purpose of the robot is to guide the movement of the operating head along a predetermined path. The robot of *Fig. 7.5a* has six axes about which movement can take place. (By comparison the human arm/

178

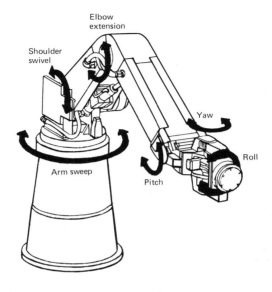

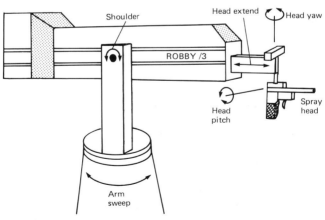

Figure 7.5. Robots. *(a)* Fully-articulated robot. *(b)* Paint-spraying robot

hand has nine basic axes). Usually six axes are adequate for painting and welding. For simpler transfer robots, four or five axes will often suffice. Each axis must have some form of actuator to provide the force for motion about the axis, and some form of positional, or angular, measuring device. The actuators are usually an ingenious combination of electric motors and hydraulic or pneumatic cylinders. Position measurement can be obtained from synchros or optical encoders. Potentiometers can be used if low-accuracy positioning is required.

Quite complicated trignometrical calculations are required to work out the current head position from the sensors at each axis. This can only be done by a computer. The calculation speed is obviously important, as the head position needs to be measured continuously.

Once the robot can calculate the head position in space, it is next necessary to have the head follow a predetermined path. Each and every axis must have its own closed-loop position control. Usually the control computer forms part of the loop as described for *Fig. 5.19*.

The required path can be described in co-ordinate form by a programming panel or, more commonly, by using a human instructor. Most robots can be taught by an operator guiding the head over the required route. The robot continuously reads and records the positions of each axis and will then faithfully repeat the operator's actions (including, it should be noted, his mistakes!).

There are many reasons for using robots. A reasonable approximation is to equate one robot with one job, but this will obviously increase on a three-shift basis to nearer four jobs. There is also a very real gain in productivity. A production line welder rarely works for more than 35 per cent of the time. This is not due to any laziness; no human being can concentrate 100 per cent of the time. After meal breaks, most time is lost in many small lapses of concentration, each of only a few seconds, but together forming a large part of a working day. Robots can achieve useful work for around 95 per cent of the time, the down time being mainly caused by routine maintenance.

180

There are also social factors to be considered (although few firms would consider robots on other than economic grounds). Many jobs which are dirty, dangerous or monotonous are ideally suited for robot operation. A robot will work continuously, without complaint, for 24 hours a day in hot, dusty and noisy conditions, and there will be no visits from the factory inspector if a robot gets burnt by a molten metal spillage.

If there are so many advantages in using robots, it is reasonable to ask why there are so few in operation. If a robot can replace four jobs, it is not going to be welcomed by the unions. It is probable that this understandable resistance from the workforce is the biggest obstacle to the introduction of robots.

Robots do, however, have some quite serious shortcomings. A robot can only position its head to about 0.5 mm. In addition, all robots at present work open-loop; a rod can only be placed in a hole if the hole is precisely placed on the work table, and there is adequate clearance between the rod and hole to accommodate the head-positioning error. A human would observe the rod approaching the hole and correct the rod position. The final insertion would be done by feel, and can accommodate an interference fit.

A human operator can deal with components arriving on a conveyor belt at any angle or position. A robot can only deal with accurately placed objects. Often the costs of the changes to the delivery system will greatly exceed the costs of the robot itself. Development work is underway to give robots rudimentary sight and tactile sensors, but it will be some time before production robots will be equipped with them. Costs will, of course, rise with the additional features.

Robots are best suited to well-defined routine jobs where the job 'environment' can be rigorously controlled. Human being are needed where flexibility and observation are essential and the job content cannot be accurately predicted. Fortunately, the jobs robots do best are those least liked by humans, so union fears of mass unemployment may prove unfounded.

Industrial control

The use of the microcomputer for control was discussed briefly in Chapter 5. To see how these ideas are put into practice we shall look at the GEC GEM-80 system shown in *Fig. 7.6*. The basic computer system comprises a single 19-inch rack, and visually bears little resemblance to preconceived ideas of a computer; no flashing lights, no whirling tape units.

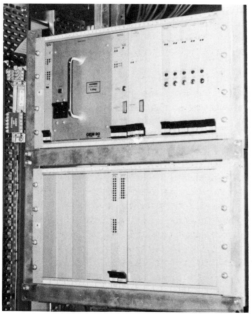

Figure 7.6. The GEM-80 industrial control computer

At the left-hand side of the unit is the power supply. Physically the largest item in the assembly, the power supply is quite complex, containing self-test logic, limit trips and power-up, power-down sequencing. The watchdog protection is also included in the power supply unit.

The next unit is the processor itself, built around the Intel 8085. Although the 8085 is an eight-bit micro, the system has been designed to be compatible with future 16-bit micros as these become available. To aid this compatibility, the 8085 is aided by an AMD super-arithmetic chip which provides 16-bit multiply and divide functions and, to some extent, makes the 8085 look like a 16-bit micro. The processor has its own scratchpad RAM, and the interpreter for the rather unique programming language is held in PROMs.

Next to the processor is the VDU board. This is, itself, a small microcomputer driving a colour VDU. The VDU is not limited to a single display format; most applications will require several 'pages' (e.g. animated plant mimics in over-view and detailed displays, alarm messages, history record-ing).

The many VDU formats and the plant control program are held in 8K static RAM boards. The number of boards will depend on the system complexity; the unit in *Fig. 7.6* has two boards for the video formats, and three for the system program.

Finally, on the lower rack are the analog input and output boards. These communicate with the processor by an intelli-gent fast I/O driver board.

Digital inputs and outputs are connected to the processor via ribbon cables. No great attempt has been made to miniaturise the plant termination panels as quite heavy cabling is used for industrial control. Plant connections are made to termination panels similar to *Fig. 7.7*. These termina-tion panels connect back to the GEM-80 via daisy-chained ribbon cables, visible at the right of the photograph.

Digital input and output blocks plug into the termination panels. These blocks contain the opto-isolation and interface logic. Blocks are available for a wide range of voltages, both AC and DC.

The basic GEM-80 system can be represented by *Fig. 7.8*. Up to eight termination panels can be connected to each ribbon. Each termination panel can handle 32 inputs or outputs, so a single processor can communicate with 512 digital inputs or outputs.

Serial ports are provided for printers and similar devices. These serial ports can also be used to build a control system based on several GEM-80s. Where a plant covers a large area, cabling costs can become excessive, and it usually becomes cheaper (and more logical) to provide a computer for each area and send data between them via serial links. The serial links can be up to 5 km in length and can operate at 9600 baud. More than two processors can be connected on to one link to provide quite extensive computer networks.

Figure 7.7. The (surprisingly large) plant connections on a control computer

The video processor, central processor and fast I/O logic all require access to the control, data and address buses shown in *Fig. 7.8*. Bus control logic (known as bus arbitration) is needed to prevent clashes. A processor requiring access to the bus sends a bus request signal to the control logic. If the buses are free, the control logic responds with a bus grant which gives control of the buses to the initialising processor.

The GEM-80 is programmed with a rather unique, but easy to learn, language based on relay terminology. Each plant connection has a unique reference. A3.14, for example, is a digital input connected to terminal 14 on termination panel 3.

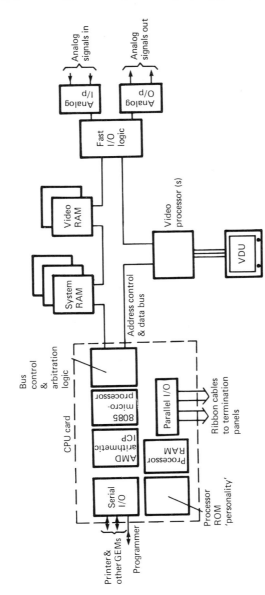

Figure 7.8. GEM-80 block diagram

185

For simple controls, relay symbols are used to define the relationship between plant inputs and outputs. *Fig. 7.9* shows a simple program for driving a two-way hydraulic cylinder. The program is understandable to any competent electrician.

The programming language is not limited to simple relay schemes, though. A comprehensive range of functions is included for arithmetic operations on analog functions, and common control operations such as PID (three-term control) feedback loops. *Fig. 7.10* shows a three-term control loop, where C128 is the controlled variable measured by one channel on the analog I/O, and D195 is the controlling actuator. The PID variables (gain, integral and differential times) are held in preset tables in the memory and can easily be tweaked by the maintenance technicians.

The GEM-80 is programmed by the portable programmer shown in *Fig. 7.11*. This displays the program on its VDU screen in the form of *Figs. 7.9* and *7.10*. The programmer connects to the central processor via its own serial link. Comprehensive monitoring of the plant operations can also be performed with the programmer, which simplifies fault finding considerably. In addition all inputs and outputs are monitored by LEDs on the termination panel blocks.

The user programs (known as ladder diagrams) are stored on cassettes, and loaded using the portable programmer and a normal domestic cassette recorder. A complete program can be loaded in 15 minutes (just long enough to make and drink a cup of coffee!)

The designers of the GEM-80 appreciated that most first-line maintenance is done by non-technical personnel, and they accordingly included self-test facilities into the processor. At start-up, and at regular intervals during operation, the processor conducts test routines on itself and the other items of *Fig. 7.8*. If the plant is designed such that every output produces a limit switch input, and analog loops are modelled in the program, the system can communicate all faults in English (e.g. No. 3 air damper failed to open; or CRC fault on RAM board 5). The processor should be able to direct the technicians to a replaceable unit such as an electronic board or a plant actuator/limit switch directly.

186

```
                    G.E.C.  ELECTRICAL PROJECTS LTD.          PAGE    1
                    G.E.C.  INDUSTRIAL CONTROLS LTD.

                    DEMONSTRATION PROGRAM FOR SIMPLE HYDRAULIC CYLINDER
                    PREPARED FOR BEGINNERS GUIDE TO MICROPROCESSORS BY E.A. PARR

GEM80 MICRO-CONTROLLER LADDER DIAGRAM

THE INSTRUCTION-NUMBER OF EACH COIL IS SHOWN BELOW IT
INSTRUCTIONS END AT NUMBER    11

   OUTPB    TOPLIM   INCOIL                                          OUTCOIL
  --]  [--+--]  [------]/[----------------------------------------  --(  )-+
   A1.12 |  A1.13     B2.1                                            B2.0  |
         |                                                          (   5  )
  |OUTCOIL|                                                         USED:-  |
  +--]  [--+                                                           5    |
   B2.0                                                               11    |

  |BACKPB   BOTMLIM  OUTCOIL                                         INCOIL |
  --]  [--+--]  [------]/[----------------------------------------  --(  )-+
   A1.11 |  A1.14     B2.0                                            B2.1  |
         |                                                          (  11  )
  |INCOIL |                                                         USED:-  |
  +--]  [--+                                                           5    |
   B2.1                                                               11    |
```

Figure 7.9. Industrial sequence program. 'A' refers to inputs, 'B' to outputs

187

```
G.E.C.  ELECTRICAL PROJECTS LTD.
G.E.C.  INDUSTRIAL CONTROLS LTD.

     DEMONSTRATION THREE TERM CONTROLLER
     FOR BEGINNERS GUIDE TO MICROPROCESSORS      E. A. PARR

GEM80 MICRO-CONTROLLER LADDER DIAGRAM

THE INSTRUCTION-NUMBER OF EACH COIL IS SHOWN BELOW IT
INSTRUCTIONS END AT NUMBER   7

! SETPT                  PIDABS    GAINETC                        ACTUATR
+-<AND>-----------------<SUB>---SPEC.---VALUE-------------------<OUT>+
! C127                            S34      P31                    D195  !
                          >    >                                  <  7  !
                          >  -<                                         !
! ACTUAL LINCON FACTORS!  +-<                                           !
+-<AND>---SPEC.---VALUE-+                                               !
! C128      S11     P32                                                 !
```

Figure 7.10. Three-term (PID) control program. Location P32 contains the conversion factors for the AX + B linear conversion. Location P31 contains the gain, integral time, differential time for the PID function

There are many add-on devices that simplify the design and installation of a control system. Contact scanners and lamp drivers (built on the principle of *Fig. 4.24*) can be daisy-chained on to a ribbon cable. This allows an entire control desk to be built and tested at the factory, and simply be

Figure 7.11. GEM-80 portable programmer (Photo: GEC)

'plugged-in' on site. Other add-ons include intelligent position controllers and remote I/O (allowing termination panels to be mounted up to 5 kilometres from the processor). Control applications range from simple machine-tool sequences to complete process control. The GEM-80 range of control computers and peripherals allows the control engineer to tailor his control system exactly to his needs. The expandability of the system makes any future extension very easy to implement.

Word processors

The word processor is one of the current growth areas in microcomputers. Heralded as the precursor of the electronic office of the future, a word processor installation meets all the requirements for a successful microcomputer application; high economic benefits, simple software that will be identical for each customer, and minimal installation costs.

In its simplest form a word processor replaces the typewriter by a VDU and keyboard connected to a microcomputer and printer, as shown in *Fig. 7.12*. Text is typed into the VDU, and stored in the computer. The VDU display can be considered as a window on this text, and control keys are used to move the window up and down the text.

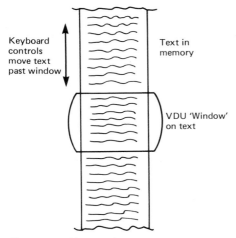

Figure 7.12. The word processor

Typing errors and text modifications can be dealt with easily. The requisite portion of text is brought to the VDU window, and corrections made by insertions, deletions or overwriting of characters. The processor shuffles all succeeding text to ensure no words are split between lines. When this editing is complete, the final text can be sent to a printer.

This simple application would suit a secretary, but most word processors offer far more facilities than simple text entry, editing and printing. Most firms use many standard letters. A master letter will be held for each of these on the word processor disc storage. To send a standard letter, the typist calls the master and enters the details required to personalise it.

For example, a standard blank could be:

```
XX1
XX2
XX3
XX4
```

```
Dear XX1
We are writing in connection with your application
for the post of XX5.  You are requested to attend
for interview on XX6 at XX7.  Please indicate if
this is convenient.  Upon arrival please report to
XX8.
(Option 1)  Second class rail fare and reasonable
meal expenses will be refunded.
(Option 2)  We note that your attendance will
require an overnight stay, and have accordingly
reserved accommodation at XX9.
Yours sincerely
```

The blank text would be displayed with a prompt list for the text inserts XX1 to 9 and the two options, for example:

```
XX8?         Security Gate 3
Options?     1 & 2
XX9?         Post House Hotel, Cambusnethan Road
```

Standard letter production is obviously a great time-saver for the typing pool, and could easily be extended to the production of contracts and other legal documents. Unfortunately the legal profession seems very slow to adopt the technology.

The advertising profession have been very quick to realise the potential of the personalised letter, and by mixing data bank files with the word processor, it is possible to annoy people with 'Dear Mr Parr, today fortune smiles on the town of Carluke. You are amongst our favoured customers in Lanarkshire who qualify for a special offer . . . .'. The advertising applications are, at worst, humorous but many people expressed concern when a political organisation in the USA used similar techniques to tailor recruiting letters to the recipients' inclinations and beliefs.

Text from a word processor is aesthetically very pleasing, being neat, uniform and often justified to align left and right margins. Centralisation of headings can be easily achieved automatically. Daisywheel printers are usual, although matrix printers are found in cheaper installations.

A useful side effect of a word processor installation is the virtual disappearance of the office filing cabinet. All letters are stored on disc or tape, and can be found quickly. Interestingly, where two offices are equipped with word processors, it would be technically feasible to dispense totally with the paper stage and transmit all correspondence between them electronically. Incoming and outgoing mail

Figure 7.13. A commercial word processing installation. The computer/disc unit is in the glass office (Photo: 'Steel News')

could both be stored on disc, and displayed on a VDU screen when required. A few firms have used similar systems for internal memos, but there have been few applications between firms. It is quite possible that the word processor could be the first stage in the disappearance of the postman.

The electronic newspaper compositor uses the same technology as the word processor, but the finished product is the plates for the printing presses. The saga of the microprocessor's introduction into the newspaper industry has been long and sad, combining heavy-handed management and union intransigence. Future historians discussing the second industrial revolution will probably use the printing industry as a case study of what went wrong.

Small business computers

Most owners of small firms complain about the long hours they have to spend on a dreary trail of paperwork: salaries, income tax, VAT, stock control, chasing debtors, and so on. This time is, to them, really wasted as it is time they could usefully spend running their businesses.

A small computer system comprising a microcomputer with about 32K RAM, two floppy discs and a printer similar to *Fig. 7.14* will cost about half of a typist's annual salary, and should be able to relieve the businessman of many of these chores. In any computer magazine there are literally hundreds of firms offering programs for payroll, stock control, etc., at very low prices, but for the inexperienced first-time buyer it can be like walking through a minefield.

The difference between buying a computer system in the traditional manner (where a systems analyst from a computer firm would plan a program for you) and buying a microcomputer program is similar to buying a made-to-measure suit and an off-the-peg suit. The former is tailored specifically to your needs, the latter fits where it touches, and the price is adjusted accordingly.

Off-the-peg business programs must, if they are to be cheap, be very general-purpose so it may be difficult to find one that meets your requirements. Quite a few people have found that they have had to modify their way of running their business to suit the computer rather than the other way round. In some respects this may be no bad thing, as firms do tend to get in a rut.

Another problem can occur when you run into difficulties. A cynical description of a 'fully-tested program' often given is 'quite a few of the errors have been removed'. If you have a payroll program that you bought for £50 which six months later totally erases all your figures, what sort of assistance can you reasonably expect?

Figure 7.14. Small business machine with 2 discs and printer (Photo: Commodore Business Machines)

The majority of commercial programs are well written, but it is a lucrative market and there are inevitably a few cowboys around. Some programs the author has seen have been abysmal. Business programs should be written in such a manner that improbable data is queried (more than 20 hours'

194

overtime in a week, for example) and no user action can cause the program to crash. This is known as defensive programming, and is sadly lacking in the worst programs. A useful test is to try entering 31st September as a date. If the program accepts it, *beware!*

Another point to watch is how much backup protection is needed. Computers do fail; not very often, but once can be too much. If your computer fails in the middle of a payroll run, or the CEGB pull the plug in the middle of a disc transfer what happens? Ideally you should only have to go back to the start of the current operation, but on some badly written programs all your records could be lost.

It may be thought that this section has been very negative. The small business machine has all the requirements for a successful microcomputer application; large benefits, minimal installation costs, and many users so programming costs can be spread. Unfortunately many people have been carried away on a wave of initial enthusiasm and installed systems which hindered, rather than helped, their businesses.

It is quite easy to introduce a computer into a small firm if several elementary precautions are taken.

a. Don't try to write your own program unless you have considerable experience.

b. Don't rely on a friend's son who's just done a course on computer studies at the local tech. Writing defensive programs needs experience, and a one-off program will inevitably contain bugs that your friend's son might not be keen to come and cure once his enthusiasm has worn off.

c. Look carefully at the way the business is run at present. Can it be streamlined without a computer?

d. If possible, try to visit users of the computer and software you are interested in and see what they think.

e. Buy the computer and software as a package from a recognised dealer. All the large manufacturers (Commodore, Apple etc) have approved-dealer networks and approved program suppliers. Buying this way improves your after-sales service considerably.

f. Establish what assistance you will get in introducing the computer into your business. Some firms' assistance ends when you walk out of the shop. Better firms will help you get started and deal with your (inevitable) problems.

g. Find what backup protection is needed for your records. Don't believe salesmen who say their computers never go wrong.

h. Be prepared to alter your procedures somewhat to suit an off-the shelf program unless you have the money for a custom-written program.

i. Try to assess how much time it will take each day to run your program. Many early users discovered their paperwork took longer with the computer than without.

j. Don't be impressed, or frightened, by computer jargon.

The small business computer can be a great boon, and will probably be the real growth area of the next decade. Fortunately, most suppliers have realised the early mistakes. Most computers are introduced with little trauma and great benefits, but the rule must be 'take care!'.

The home computer

It is now possible for an outlay of under £100 to become the owner of a home computer. It would seem likely that in the near future the home computer will become as common as the TV set.

There are really two categories of home computers. The first is the hobby, or kit, computer which is aimed at the electronic enthusiast. These are kits which take some time, and no little skill, to complete. Usually compromising a naked set of printed circuit boards they are ideal for people who like to tinker with the electronics and build add-on circuits such as music boxes or ADCs.

The second category is the ready-made computer, covering the Sinclair ZX81 at the bottom end to the full-colour Apple with a price difference of one to ten. All that these machines require is a mains plug. They are consequently well suited to a newcomer's needs, who will be more interested in learning progamming than chasing an intermittent fault on a RAM board.

These machines all have great similarities. They usually consist of the computer, a full typewriter keyboard and a VDU. Often, to save cost, a modulated video output is provided to allow a domestic TV to be used as the VDU. Program storage is done on a standard cassette recorder. Most machines use BASIC, which is the ideal language for the novice. One cautionary point, however, is that some Tiny BASICs (or integer BASICs) only deal in whole numbers, so 13/6 would give the result 2.

Figure 7.15. The extremes of the home computer market: the Hewlett Packard 9845 and the Sinclair ZX80

As the owner's skills progress, it is usual to buy additional facilities, the commonest being printers, discs and extra memory. These lift the machine out of the toy category and into the samll business machine class.

The home computer is supposed to have many uses around the home; keeping track of the home accounts, helping the kids with the homework, keeping check on the freezer contents and so on. In most cases, the author

197

suspects, these are excuses for buying the machine and not the real reason.

Computer programming is a tremendous intellectual challenge similar to chess, and most home computer owners view their machines in the same way as model railways or any other hobby; i.e. an end in itself and not something that needs to be specifically useful. Home computers can keep records of your bank account, or work out your motoring costs, but in most households the back of an envelope will do the job as well.

Using the computer to control things is also difficult to implement. Home computers can be made to control your central heating, feed the cat or water your plants, but such exercises are usually trivial and not worth the effort and expense involved.

Children take to computers like ducks to water, and their education is a very good reason for having a home computer. Even playing games on a computer removes their natural apprehension, and most children soon want to write their own programs. In the computer-orientated world of the future, the sooner children learn how to use the machine the better. Although secondary schools are, slowly, becoming equipped with computers it will be a long time before the average child can get adequate time at a keyboard in school. The home computer can provide this much needed experience.

Any home computer owner should join a computer club. Some, such as the Amateur Computer Club, are general clubs; others such as the INMC (for Nascom users,) are dedicated to a specific machine. These clubs offer a lively medium for the interchange of programs and ideas. Secretaries change frequently, but the computer magazines publish lists at regular intervals.

The white goods market

Buried deep inside washing machines, tumbler driers and dishwashers is a complex bit of electro-mechanical machinery called a programmer. Comprising at least one small electric motor and many cams, switches, levers and springs, it is both the most expensive, and unreliable, part of the appliance.

The programmer is required to control the operation of the appliance, and follows a very simple sequence, usually of the form 'Wait until the water reaches limit switch 3 then close valve 4 and move on to the next step'. This is obviously a job that could easily be done by a microcomputer.

Single-chip computers such as the TMS 1000 described earlier are ideally suited to domestic appliances with their high production runs. The chip cannot itself replace the entire programmer. Additional devices such as triacs will be needed to drive motors, etc., and the whole circuit will need to be mounted on a printed circuit board (PCB) and provided with a power supply.

Despite these additional costs (which will increase the programmer cost to about six times the cost of the actual microcomputer) it is still far cheaper than the electro-mechanical programmer. The major cost saving comes from the considerable labour costs involved in building electro-mechanical versions.

The electronic programmer has no moving parts, and should prove very reliable. If a failure does occur, replacement of the programmer PCB will be easy and cheap.

Microprocessor-based dishwashers, cookers and washing machines are already available and are proving very reliable. Initially, these have been in the 'up-market' ranges, but it seems likely that sheer economics will lead to their introduction in popular models as well.

Automobiles

Electronics has been slow to be accepted by the automobile industry, the average car's electrical system being largely unchanged from the 1930s. Interest is being shown, however, in microcomputers, and several manufacturers are designing micros into the next generation of cars.

As fuel costs rise, fuel economy becomes more important. One of the most interesting developments is the electronic control of air/fuel ratio and ignition timing by a microcomputer. This system requires eight engine sensors, and works out ideal settings from a 'model' of the engine held in ROM. A particular feature is the ability to switch out cylinders when the engine is idling or running free. Although not cheap, increasing fuel prices and more stringent US legislation on exhaust emissions will probably cause engine computers to be fitted to production cars in the not too distant future.

Anti-skid devices have been around for some time, but their cost has meant that they have only been fitted to articulated vehicles. Micro-based systems have been developed, but at present they are restricted by the cost of the sensors used to measure road speed and wheel rotation. The public has never shown itself willing to pay for safety features unless forced by legislation, so it is unlikely that antiskid systems will be fitted unless required by law.

Some of the proposed applications border, frankly, on the ludicrous. A prototype Ford Lincoln has been produced with a bank of digital displays and a speech synthesiser chip giving audible warnings to the driver. The author's personal view is that the current 'analogue' indication on a car dash panel conveys information quite satisfactorily, and this particular application is an excellent example of the micro looking for something silly to do.

Electronic circuits in an automobile have a particularly hard time. The battery supply can vary from 9 volts to 15 volts, and can carry 1 kV pulses as a starter motor disengages. Under-bonnet temperatures can easily span the full military temperature range of $-55°C$ to $+125°C$. The whole circuit has to be sealed against the ingress of moisture. The physical and electrical protection of any automobile microcomputer will therefore be a large part of the cost.

8

The micro and the future

'It is desirable to guard against the possibility of exaggerated ideas that might arise as to the powers of the Analytical Engine. In considering any new subject there is frequently a tendency, first, to *overrate* what we find already to be interesting or remarkable; and secondly, by a sort of natural reaction, to *undervalue* the true state of the case, when we do discover that our notions have surpassed those that were really tenable'.

The words above were written in the early 19th century by Ada Augusta, the Countess of Lovelace, whilst describing Charles Babbage's remarkable Analytical Engine. It seems that her words are still valid today, because the media are at the first stage of overrating the microprocessor's capabilities and effects and professional computer engineers have progressed to the second stage. Some people have gone as far as to say 'Microprocessors have put back computing by at least 10 years'.

The truth, of course, lies between the two extremes, and the reader should now be in a position to decide what is feasible and what is not.

The microprocessors described in this book have been a snapshot of the early 1980s, and as development is continuous the microprocessor will undoubtedly improve. In the rest of this chapter we look at some technical developments that are likely to occur in the near future, and consider a few views of the computer-run world of the latter part of this century.

Sixteen-bit microprocessors

The eight-bit word length of the common microcomputers is a major restriction, and most microcomputers approximate to minicomputers such as the PDP8 from the 1960s. As integrated circuit technology improved and Very Large Scale Integration (VLSI) became economically practical, it was

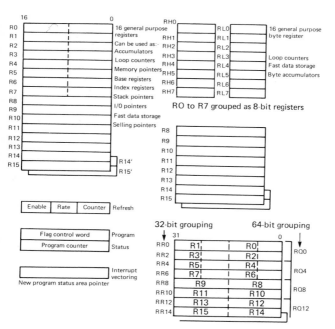

Figure 8.1. Z-8000 register configurations

inevitable that the next generation of microprocessors would be 16-bit machines of similar power to popular minicomputers such as the PDP11. These 16-bit microprocessors are, like their smaller eight-bit brothers, the CPU of a computer; the user still has to supply ROM, RAM, and I/O.

To appreciate how a 16-bit microprocessor is used, we shall look at the Zilog Z-8000 series. The programmer's model is shown in *Fig. 8.1*. There are 16 general-purpose 16-bit registers, which are all truly general purpose. All registers can be used as accumulators, counters, stack pointers, index registers or memory pointers (for register indirect mode). These registers can also be split or grouped as in *Fig. 8.1*.

Registers R0 to R7 can be split into 16 general purpose eight-bit registers, or the full register set can be grouped into eight general purpose 32-bit registers, or four general-purpose 64-bit registers! This gives the programmer considerable flexibility in choosing his register length to suit the application. In the same program it is quite easy to use, say, an eight-bit half register to hold a simple loop counter and a 64-bit quadruple register to hold data. To call the Z-8000 a 16-bit micro is obviously an understatement!

The Z-8000 can address 8 megabytes of memory. This is achieved by dividing the address into 128 segments of up to 64K per segment. An address therefore consists of a seven-bit segment number and 16-bit address. In addition to this 'long form' (segment plus address), the Z-8000 can address directly the first 256 locations in each segment.

It is exceedingly unlikely that all 8 megabytes of memory would be RAM. In most systems there will be a 'relatively' small (about 64K) RAM, the rest of memory being located on backup stores such as discs or drums. As programs or data are required, they are brought down from the disc to the RAM. This technique, known as Virtual Memory, can be a burden to the CPU, but most manufacturers provide Memory Management Units (MMUs) to relieve the processor of the operation.

The MMU is connected between the CPU and memory as shown in *Fig. 8.2*. As far as the processor is concerned, all memory is held in RAM. If the processor calls for data on the disc, the MMU asks the processor to wait, stores the current RAM contents on to the disc for safety, brings the required data to the RAM, then signals that the processor can continue. This shuffle is performed solely by the MMU without any intervention by the processor.

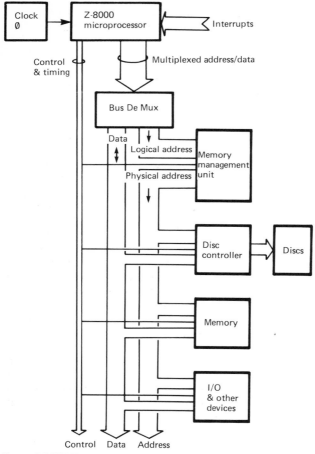

Figure 8.2 Z8000 system with memory management

The MMU has other important facilities. In earlier chapters we saw that a CPU does not know the difference between RAM data and RAM instructions, and can easily go off the rails if a programming error directs the program to a wrong part of the store. With an MMU, areas of store can be designated 'Data' or 'Program' and can only be accessed in the correct section of the Fetch/Execute/Reset cycle outlined in Chapter 1.

It is envisaged that these 16-bit micros will be used in multi-task systems where many programs run 'simultaneously' on the same machine under the control of a supervisory program. The MMU can be used to 'lock-off' areas of the memory so that one of the multi-task programs cannot wander off outside its own memory area. Similar protection can be given to multiprocessor systems where several CPUs share memory.

Once the necessary complexity of the instruction set has been mastered, programming a 16-bit micro should be easier than the eight-bit generation. Most include multiply and divide to 32-bit accuracy. The comprehensive register set simplifies data movement. Despite this the eight-bit micro user should experience no great trauma; programming a 16-bit micro is merely an extension of eight-bit ideas. The Z-8000 uses eight addressing modes; Register, Immediate, Register Indirect, Direct, Indexed, Relative, Base and Base Indexed. There are nine categories of instruction: Loads and moves, Arithmetic, Logic, Program Control, Bit manipulation, Rotates and Shifts, Block Transfer, Input/Output, CPU control. The address modes and instructions should be familiar to the eight-bit user.

The Z-8000 comes, surprisingly, in the same 40-pin DIL i.c.p. as the 8-bit Z-80. This is achieved by using a multiplexed address/data bus in a similar manner to the 8085 described in Chapter 6. RAM and I/O designed for use with the Z-8000 incorporate their own address/data demultiplexer. Other items can be used with an external demultiplexer.

There are many support i.c.p.s for the Z-8000; DMA controllers, disc controllers, timers, etc. These allow a system designer to 'bolt together' his system.

We have described the Z-8000 as a typical 16-bit microprocessor. All the major manufacturers have their own versions. Motorola have the 68000 which uses a development of the 6800/6809 (the 6800 instruction set is a subset of the 68000 set). Intel have the 8086, and Texas Instruments the 9900.

Designers of TV games will find the National Semiconductor 16016, designed for the arcade market, of interest. These all have their own quirks and advantages, but are basically similar to the Z-8000.

Sixteen-bit micros are not cheap; at the time of writing a Z-8000 costs more than a complete microcomputer based on an 8-bit micro. In addition, the store is twice as expensive as each location holds a 16-bit word. If the history of the eight-bit micro is repeated, costs should fall dramatically.

The 16-bit micro is just another step in the evolution of the computer. Designers are now talking of the 32-bit micro. Watch this space . . . .

The bubble memory

Any computer system designer soon realises that many systems require storage that is prohibitively expensive to provide in RAM, but need access times faster than that provided by discs. This need for a relatively fast bulk storage system may be met by an interesting development known as the 'bubble memory'.

In some materials, magnetic domains are formed which have a preferred line of magnetisation. For convenience we will call the two possible directions 'up' and 'down'. Normally the material has random stripes of magnetisation similar to *Fig. 8.3a*. If a magnetic field is applied as in *Fig. 8.3b*, the antiparallel regions shrink until, at a certain critical field strength, small magnetic bubbles are left as shown in *Fig. 8.3c*. These bubbles are mobile and can be moved around by suitable magnetic fields. It should be noted that no material moves, it is simply the magnetisation that is mobile.

To use these bubbles for storage, they must be controlled. There are many ways of achieving this, but the simplest to understand is the structure of *Fig. 8.4*. Magnetically soft nickel iron is deposited on the surface of the material in the shape of alternate I and T formations. A bias field is applied perpendicular to the paper to allow bubbles to form, and a rotating field applied in the plane of the paper. As the field rotates, the I and T elements are magnetised in sympathy, and simple magnetic attraction and repulsion shifts the bubble one place to the right for each field rotation.

Bubbles are generated by a small current loop, and sensed by a Hall-effect probe or magnetostrictive device. In its simplest form, a bubble memory is a very large shift register.

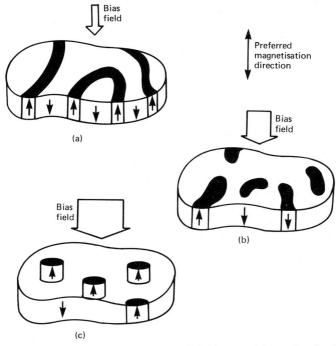

Figure 8.3 Magnetic bubbles. *(a)* Small field, striped form. *(b)* Islands formed. *(c)* Islands become cylindrical bubbles

Serially-accessed devices such as this have an inherent delay in reading data because the computer has to wait for the data to go round the loop. The delay can be reduced considerably by adopting a major/minor loop arrangement similar to *Fig. 8.5.* Data is loaded serially on to the major loop in blocks of,

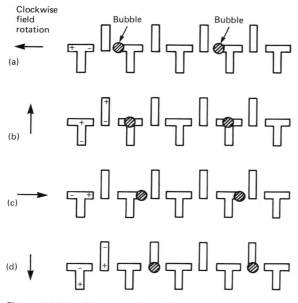

Figure 8.4. T and I propagation elements

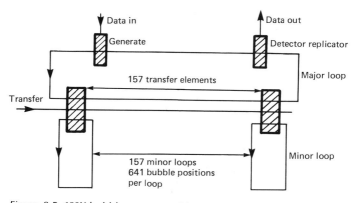

Figure 8.5. 100K bubble memory with major/minor loops

say, 150 bits. At the end of each block, a parallel transfer is made on to the 150 minor loops. The data now circulates round the minor loops, each of which has about 700 positions per loop. To read data, a maximum of 700 field rotations is needed to bring the data back to the transfer position where it can be transferred back to the major loop. Another 150 field rotations brings all the data block out in serial form. The device in *Fig. 8.5* will store 100K bits with an access time under 1 ms.

The construction of a typical bubble memory is shown in *Fig. 8.6*. The bias field is provided by two permanent magnets, and the rotating field by two coils driven by sine waves

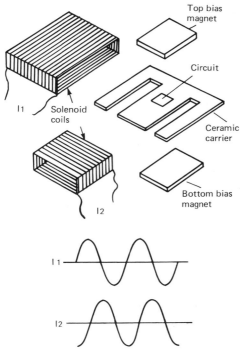

Figure 8.6. Bubble memory chip

90 degrees out of phase. The circuit itself sits on a small ceramic carrier inside the coils.

Bubble memories are non-volatile, which removes the need for the awkward refresh logic and batteries of semiconductor RAM boards. Access times are faster than discs, so the bubble fits conveniently in the gap between fast RAM and slow discs. Current devices have a capacity of 100K bits. It is expected that 8M-bit devices will be available by the mid 1980s. Amateurs interested in bubble memories will be pleased to know that bubble memories are becoming available for hobby computers, the first being a 100K-bit device for the Nascom computer based on the Texas Instruments bubble memory.

Networking & Telesoftware

Microcomputers are becoming increasingly common in schools and colleges. It rapidly became apparent that expensive items such as disc drives and printers are used by an individual microcomputer user relatively infrequently and could be shared between machines. From this grew the idea of 'networking', where a cluster of machines could be connected to each other, to common resources or even to a larger mainframe computer.

Networking is not limited to the classroom, however. Using modems (see Chapter 4) computers can be connected over continents, to exchange programs and information. It is likely that in the not too distant future you will be able to see what is in stock at your supermarket, check your bank balance or renew your library books from a home computer terminal.

A related, but one-way, transmission method is Telesoftware, currently undergoing trials in the UK. The Teletext service offered by the BBC (as Ceefax) and ITV (as Oracle) has the capacity to transmit complete computer programs which can be received and stored in a home computer. Similar services are likely to be included in British Telecom's Prestel system.

The array processor

It was mentioned in Chapter 1 that every computer built has the block diagram of *Fig. 1.2*. This model, known as the Von Neumann machine, is only one of several ways in which a computer could be constructed, the others being unknown outside university research departments.

The Von Neumann machine is used as the basis of all computers because it is the simplest to implement. The arrival of the microprocessor has made other approaches feasible, and a technique known as 'array processing' seems likely to emerge from the research departments as a commercial reality.

A conventional computer is rather similar to an assembly line; the program works in a logical sequence along the predetermined set of instructions doing one task at a time. An array processor, as its name implies, consists of an aray of processors capable of doing many tasks in parallel. Machines built to date utilise an array of 64 × 64 processors controlled by a master processor. The array processor is thus similar to an assembly shop rather than an assembly line.

Not all problems are really suitable for an array processor, the majority of applications having been in areas where there is a lot of similar data to be processed. Particularly impressive are the computer-enhanced pictures from NASA which use array-processing techniques.

Array processors are phenomenally expensive, so it is unlikely that it will be an area of interest to the amateur in the foreseeable future.

Limits to size

The slices on which integrated circuits are made are small for reasons of economics and speed. A rough indication of a device's 'computing power' is given by the product of the number of elements and the speed. The speed of a device is inversely proportional to the size of the logic elements and the number of elements that can be fitted on a given slice is inversely proportional to the size of the logic elements and the number of elements that can be fitted on a given slice is inversely proportional to the square of the element size. It follows, by simple mathematics, that halving the element size leads to an eight-fold increase in 'power'.

Given this rather frightening thought, it is reasonable to ask what decrease in the element size can be foreseen from the current state of the art. Element size is usually measured in terms of the width of the basic transistors and resistors, called the line width. Currently, line widths of the order of 4 µm are being used. (At that thickness, railway lines could be drawn up the edge of the paper of one page of this book.) It is widely thought that devices can be made with a line width of 0.1 µm before quantum effects (which cause electrons to stop behaving predictably) become apparent. This represents a 40-fold improvement on today's devices and an incredible 64 000 times increase in 'power'.

Whether this density can be achieved is open to some question. Yields of 40 per cent for the eight-bit micros are considered excellent, and the figures quoted for the 16-bit micros are reputedly around 1 per cent. As the line size decreases, so the probability of misregistration, dust, and impurities causing a faulty device, rises. It may be that the law of diminishing returns will set in before the theoretical 0.1 µm line width is reached.

Another very real problem concerns testing. It is interesting to note that manufacturers are unable to test totally today's eight-bit micros; in the time available only a few vital functions can be monitored. As devices increase in complexity, it will be a very real problem to know if your new superchip is working correctly or not!

Appendix

Number systems

In everyday life we use a decimal number system, and there is a tendency to assume that this is the 'natural' way to count. In reality, a number system can be constructed to any base, and we use a decimal (ten based) system because we have ten fingers.

In a decimal system we use powers of ten. The number 8759, for example, means:

	8 thousands	=	$8 \times 10 \times 10 \times 10$
plus	7 hundreds	=	$7 \times 10 \times 10$
plus	5 tens	=	5×10
plus	9 ones	=	9

Three number systems are encountered in computing: hexadecimal or hex (to base sixteen), octal (to base 8) and binary (to base 2). Hex and octal are used because they are a shorthand way of representing binary as explained in Chapter 3.

Our decimal system uses ten symbols, the numbers 0 to 9. It follows that hex uses sixteen symbols (0–9, A, B, C, D, E, F), octal uses eight symbols (0–7), and binary just two (0, 1). As we saw above, positions in a number represent powers. For example, in hex C7A means:

	C	(twelve)	$\times 16 \times 16$	=	3072	in decimal
plus	7		$\times 16$	=	112	in decimal
plus	A	(ten)	$\times 1$	=	10	in decimal
					3194	in decimal

The octal number 6347 means:

	6 × 8 × 8 × 8	=	3072	in decimal
plus	3 × 8 × 8	=	192	in decimal
plus	4 × 8	=	32	in decimal
plus	7 × 1	=	7	in decimal
			3303	in decimal

The binary number 10110 means:

	1 × 2 × 2 × 2 × 2	=	16	in decimal
plus	0 × 2 × 2 × 2	=	0	in decimal
plus	1 × 2 × 2	=	4	in decimal
plus	1 × 2	=	2	in decimal
plus	0	=	0	in decimal
			22	in decimal

As can be seen, binary numbers become inordinately long for relatively small decimal numbers. Representation of binary numbers in hex or octal allows shortform representation while still allowing quick restoration of the original number.

Knowledge of binary, octal or hex is not normally required to program computers in BASIC or other high-level languages.

Index